MICHEL FOUCAULT: THE FREEDOM
OF PHILOSOPHY

MICHEL FOUCAULT
THE FREEDOM
OF PHILOSOPHY

John Rajchman

COLUMBIA UNIVERSITY PRESS
New York

Columbia University Press
New York   Guildford, Surrey
Copyright © 1985 Columbia University Press

Printed in the United States of America

Library of Congress Cataloging in Publication Data

Rajchman, John.
Michel Foucault, the freedom of philosophy

Includes index.
1. Foucault, Michel.   I. Title.
B2430.F724R34 1985   194   85-5895
ISBN 0-231-06070-X
ISBN 0-231-06071-8   (pa)

To Anne Boyman

Contents

MICHEL FOUCAULT: THE FREEDOM
OF PHILOSOPHY

Introduction

Disagreement, misunderstanding, and passionate controversy have long surrounded the work of Michel Foucault. It has been difficult to settle on a general consensus. There may be many reasons for this, but some of them are to be found in the very nature of Foucault's project:

1. Foucault saw to it that his work not fit within a single program; he reserved the right to always go on to something new and different. He often changed his mind and started off on new paths. He made a virtue and even an obligation of doing so. He intended to leave behind no single doctrine, method, or school of thought.

2. His work overlapped with several different disciplines without falling under the province of any one. He felt the need to question the assumptions of constituted disciplines; our disciplinary boundaries, he held, are only contingent and historical.

3. His work was disturbingly precise and concrete. The same work which was debated by analytic philosophers worried about rationality and reference was read by French prisoners worried about their living conditions. Foucault infuriated literature professors but pleased many writers and critics. His recondite reconstructions of arcane and forgotten dis-

course turned into best sellers. Foucault introduced concrete and often unsettling problems about crime, sex, madness, and disease into academic philosophical discussion; and he obliged people to reflect on those issues in new ways. His work was thus critical, practical, even political in intent. And yet it has been difficult to determine precisely what makes it so. It does not easily conform to the model of the relation of theory to practice in Marx or Freud; nor is it an instance of the philosophical attempt to recover ordinary life or language.

Because his work lacks, and was devised to avoid, the coherence of a single method or doctrine, because it falls under no single constituted discipline, and because it has a specific sort of practical or political consequence, it has led to many divergent, and often mutually inconsistent, interpretations. Foucault has been called many things he refused to call himself: a structuralist or post-structuralist, an irrationalist, a relativist, an anarchist, a nihilist.

I advance another philosophical name for his thought; it explains how these difficulties have arisen, or how they are in themselves consequences of a coherent project. The philosophical name I would give this project is not nihilism but *skepticism*. Foucault is the great skeptic of our times. He is skeptical about dogmatic unities and philosophical anthropologies. He is the philosopher of dispersion and singularity.

Sextus Empiricus is Foucault's precursor. Foucault's philosophy does not aim for sure truths, but for the freedom of withholding judgment on philosophical dogmas, and so of acquiring relief from the restrictions they introduce into our lives and our thought. He devises antithetical tropes to induce an *epoche* leading to a sort of *ataraxia* for our times; how to continue our modernist culture, our critical thought, and our politics without inherited dogmatic assumptions. Foucault directs his skeptical tropes against philosophical dogmas with which Sextus did not yet have to contend.

According to the lore of philosophy, it was Hume's skepticism about Cartesian and Lockean dogmas that awoke Kant from his slumbers. Foucault's skepticism is directed in turn against the slumbers Kant introduced; it is not simply about scholastic authority but about the certainty of systems of representation. Foucault extends Hume's doubts about the Cartesian proposition that nothing is easier for the mind to know than itself into our post-Kantian period. He presents skeptical analyses of various forms of knowledge and discourse we have invented about ourselves, analyses which suspend dogmatic postulations of a transcendental subjectivity or constitutive anthropology. When a particular conception of experience, such as our conception of mental illness, is taken for granted as natural or self-evident in a range of institutions and discourses, Foucault suspends judgment and then looks for the workings of a singular and contingent historical practice. To read Foucault is to become skeptical about the self-evidence with which it can be said that someone suffers from a mental disease, or has a criminal or homosexual personality.

Foucault induces skepticism about post-Kantian dogmas of universalist history, anthropological foundation, and master schemes. He suspends judgment about the great unified narratives of our civilization, about unified or systematic schemes for interpretation or for social change, and about the postulation of a human nature that would ground our knowledge or our political institutions. In the place of universalist narrative, he looks for the plurality and singularity of our origins; in the place of unified science or rationality, he looks for many changing practices of knowledge; in the place of a single human experience, based in our nature or in our language, he looks for the invention of specific forms of experience which are taken up and transformed again and again.

Our various sciences, languages, forms of reasoning, types of experience, structures of power and oppression are not unified timeless things. It is a kind of dogmatism to assert or assume that they must be: as though all our knowledge had to refer to a single unified world or employ a single method of reasoning; as though all our discourses had to belong to a monolithic logic or system of language with a single function; as though anything we may experience had to derive from a single structure our nature or our language prescribes for us.

Foucault is skeptical about such inherited totalities; he suggests how we might proceed without them.

Thus he does not ask classical skeptical questions about "experience in general"; he asks skeptical questions about the very idea of subsuming our sciences, rationalities, subjectivities, languages, or techniques of rule, under a single philosophical category such as "experience in general." He is skeptical not about the existence of the external world, but about the assumption that there is only one unified thing, *the* world. In his skepticism, it does not make sense to place everything in doubt at once. He does not have a total skepticism because he is skeptical about totality. Thus he does not analyze knowledge, rationality, or subjectivity in general. His skepticism proceeds case by case. It has no end; it is a permanent questioning.

His skepticism about any one case is not intended to establish certainty in some other simpler domain. He does not propose to return to the things themselves, to ordinary life or language. At the end of our dogmatic entanglements would not stand a simple and austere life. To question the self-evidence of a form of experience, knowledge, or power, is to free it for our purposes, to open new possibilities for thought or action. Such freedom is the ethical principle of Foucault's skepticism; it is what has been misunderstood as irrationalism, anarchism, or nihilism.

For it is this freedom from dogmatic unity and from the self-evidence of concrete systems of thought, which lies at the heart of Foucault's project and the difficulties peculiar to it. Foucault's skepticism is historical; it is directed against dogmatism that derives from turning a dispersed historical process into something unified and unchanging. Our unities of authorship, œuvre, and discipline present themselves as natural or grounded; yet they are historically constituted. Freedom from dogmatic unity thus leads Foucault to freedom from a unique disciplinary starting point or a single correct method. Foucault finds his skeptical freedom in belonging to no single tradition, while trying to provoke new thinking in and about many different ones. His work would begin with allegiance to no one constituted school or movement. In his singular ethic of writing without a single community, name, or following, without a fixed identity or "authorial face," it is this question of skeptical freedom that is at stake.

Skeptical freedom also determines the political intent of his analysis: what makes his analysis practical or concrete is his attempt to suspend the ahistorical naturalness through which we employ our categories of sex, mental disease, or criminality; to stop and ask about the history that stands behind such categories; to free us to imagine forms of life in which they would no longer have a constitutive role. But his political skepticism is a questioning, not an attempt to find sure truths, rational grounds, or prescriptive policies.

Foucault's skepticism started with the category of mental disease. In his first work, he withheld judgment about this category, questioned its retrospective application, and tried to find the system of thought that had made it possible. He asked what it would mean for us to live without it. (In this he parts company with Laing or Szasz; he advanced no alternative theory about the nature and treatment of mental disease.)

This skepticism found a more general philosophical ally in what a misleading shorthand has called "structuralism." Structuralism was Foucault's *crise pyrronienne*: he thought that the use of formal models in anthropology and psychoanalysis, the emergence of a modernist criticism focused on avant-garde writing, and the Bachelardian turn in the history of sciences had all denied the constitutive subject, and so had initiated a great skeptical challenge to the dogmas of philosophical anthropology that descend from Kant.

But Foucault's skepticism was to survive the idea that structuralism was the great "event" in our intellectual history. He did not sustain this view but continued his questioning of the dogmas of "anthropologism" in other more pointed and specific ways.

He remained within the general Bachelardian tradition in history of science: he devoted himself to what he called the "history of systems of thought." He refined his views on the nature of that history; Nietzsche's "genealogy" provided a model. He came to think that psychoanalysis and anthropology do not comprise a deep "break" in our thought. In *The History of Sexuality*, he redraws the map of systems of thought in such a way as to attenuate or reverse the impression of such a break. But it was primarily in a change in his attitude toward modernism that we find the break in *his* thinking.

In literary modernism, Foucault sought a romantic alternative to a culture obsessed with the principle of systematic reason and the idea of a foundational humanism. He found a madness that was not a mental disease and a writing that had fled the representational paradigm of language; the two were interconnected in a transgressive "counter-discourse." But he could not sustain this vision and abandoned his early romanticism.

In freeing himself from it, Foucault disowned the theory of language as a basis for his skeptical tropes, and the question "what is language" as the center of his history. He carried on his questioning of the subject in ways no longer based in language or structuralism. He enlarged its scope; it became less literary and more concrete.

In history, he not only questioned the constituted unities of author, work, and discipline; he also devised a new historical nominalism, and a politics of revolt in specific situations, no longer subordinated to the alternative of either revolution or reform. This raised questions about his left commitments; he reflected on the change in the nature of the engagement of the intellectual, the change from a universal to a specific role. He rethought the very nature of political critique in his challenge to what he called the "repressive hypothesis." The model of critique he devises is unlike Habermas' neo-Kantian one. His critique is not an attempt to use rational norms in a general analysis of state or society; it is rather a constant "civil disobedience" within our constituted experience.

There is a thread that runs throughout this reflection and analysis. It is what I call the question of freedom. Foucault's questioning of anthropologism turns into an ethic of free thought: in suspending universalist narrative and anthropological assurance about an abstract freedom, Foucault directs our attention to the very concrete freedom of writing, thinking, and living in a permanent questioning of those systems of thought and problematic forms of experience in which we find ourselves.

Foucault's freedom is not liberation, a process with an end. It is not liberty, a possession of each individual person. It is the motor and principle of his skepticism: the endless questioning of constituted experience. Foucault reinvents skepticism in our time through a new kind of historical analysis. It is the skepticism of our modernity; it is the question of our freedom.

Note

In "Ethics After Foucault," I discuss in detail how Foucault's practical historical skepticism is applied to the classical texts of antiquity in volumes 1 and 3 of *The History of Sexuality;* the result is a new conception of ethics.

CHAPTER ONE

The Ends of Modernism

The Swan song of Literary Theory

> The whole relentless theorization of writing which we saw in the 1960s was doubtless only a swan song. Through it the writer was fighting for the preservation of his political privilege; but the fact that it was precisely a matter of theory, that the needed scientific credentials, founded in linguistics, semiology, psychoanalysis, that this theory took its references from the direction of Saussure, of Chomsky, etc., and that it gave rise to such mediocre literary products, all this proves that the activity of the writer was no longer at the focus of things . . . we are at present experiencing the disappearance of the figure of the "great writer."[1]

So Foucault declared in a 1977 interview to preface an Italian edition of some of his essays. He tells a little "new-class" story about intellectuals in the "political not sociological sense," i.e., in terms of the uses made of knowledge and expertise in political struggles. Technical intellectuals like Oppenheimer, he explains, are replacing literary ones like Zola. The writer-intellectual tries to become a conscience for everyone; he opposes the abuse of power and wealth with universal justice and equality. One instance is the "faded" Marxist ideal of a writer articulating the universal class consciousness of the workers. The writer-intellectual is disappearing. In his place there is the university and the "specific" intellectual—specific to the particular political struggles that involve his knowledge and expertise.

It is in this context that Foucault took his brutal glance backward to the "relentless theorization of writing" in the 1960s, which, as we know, was to resurface in the American university in the 1970s and is still very much a topic of debate. Mediocre literary works, Foucault said, were clothed in epistemology, linguistics, and science, the better to survive in a technocratic culture.

What are we to make of this denunciation? I suggest it encapsulates Foucault's participation in a dramatic cultural shift: the passing of a modernist sensibility combined with an alteration in the political self-image of the intellectual. Foucault's work constitutes a diagnosis and a version of this change, and thus it is no accident that his denunciation of the avant-garde literary culture of the 1960s occurs within a story about the intellectual "in the political sense," that the crucial issue is that of knowledge and expertise (the "Enlightenment question"),[2] and that questions about "power" are said to precede those about language: "The history which bears and determines us has the form of a war rather than that of language; relations of power, not relations of meaning."[3]

Flaubert (who is the candidate of both Barthes and Foucault for the first modernist writer) perhaps first exemplifies the "antibourgeois" aims of modernist literary culture, for he envisaged a new aristocracy of letters opposed to the "revolt of the masses" and to the idea of progress, to the journalism, sentimental magazines, and middle-brow culture which were ruining the language and keeping the great writer from his sovereignty over it. In a word, Flaubert was opposed to the "mass culture" which in Europe was regularly identified with America. In 1977, when Foucault was announcing the disappearance of the writer, Barthes still saw the vocation of avant-garde writing in its opposition to "bourgeois language."[4]

The debate over *écriture* (writing) was thus a debate about the *political* culture of modernism. It was a debate about the vision of a nontechnocratic yet nonhumanistic culture that would celebrate our "decentered" relation to language in sublime laughter and "transgresssion," about an avant-garde culture (the term comes from the twenties) presenting itself as the rupture, the threshold, the limits of our age; and about a non-populist or elitist culture which was nevertheless committed to the left.

Who was thus fighting for the privileges of a political culture by theorizing about writing? Surely Barthes and the whole *nouvelle critique*. Lacan (whose *Écrits* appeared in 1966) was a central figure; it was he who transformed psychoanalysis into the great theory of modernist culture. Derrida (whose *De la grammatologie* and *L'Écriture et la différence* appeared in 1967) was the philosopher. He attempted to graft the question of writing onto the entire philosophical tradition, supplanting Heidegger's great "question of Being." In addition there were Leiris, Blanchot, Bataille, and even Beckett and some of the *nouveaux romanciers*. And, of course, there was the now defunct journal *Tel Quel*. Julia Kristeva's *Révolution du langage poétique* may someday seem a great summation of the movement. The title captures its spirit—a revolution emerging from avant-garde writing.

But one writer-intellectual notoriously obsessed throughout the 1960s with the question of writing was none other than Michel Foucault. In the 1977 interview, Foucault says that his early work was motivated by the "politics of science," the Lysenko affair, and the epistemological views of the Communist party. Yet one need only glance at his writings until the *Archaeology of Knowledge* in 1969 and his assumption of his chair at the Collège de France (and it was his most prolific period) to see that no one pursued the question of writing more relentlessly than he. Everywhere there is reference to "our" thought, "our" culture—meaning not so much we Parisians, European or Western intellectuals, as we modernists, we formalists, we who are brought together by the cultural (and therefore the political) possibilities modernist *écriture* has opened up in our era. A typical instance in *Les Mots et les choses* (1966): "The whole curiosity of our thought now resides in the question: What is language, how can we find a way around it in order to make it appear in itself, in all its plenitude . . ."[5] In short, in the 1960s, Foucault saw the emergence of a post-Enlightenment culture in modernist writing; he tried to discern the deep or archaeological possibilities from which it had come and which it augured, he specified how it was articulating the modern experience, and he brought its "sovereign laughter" into philosophy.

Literary theory in the 1960s may have been a swan song, but Foucault was part of it. His remarks are auto-biographical. They are an unspoken self-rebuke. "We" modernists did not announce a new culture; we did not even understand the politics of the old culture of which we were a part. Perhaps, then, the central questions in our era are not about commentary, language, and avant-garde art. Perhaps ours is an era of a politics of documentation, secrecy, and individuality which has made subjectivity our basic problem—our *modern* problem as political intellectuals.

Foucault's remarks in 1977 about the swan song of literary theory are symptomatic of a "break" or "rupture" in his own story. But they also indicate a more general change in which modernist culture loses its hold and in which it can no longer be taken for granted that an "engaged intellectual" is automatically *de gauche,* that his enemies are the State, the corporations, and U.S. foreign policy and culture.

It is therefore instructive to reconstruct from Foucault's own publications in the 1960s the vision of a modernist culture he now disowns, and so to determine where he must think "we" went wrong.

The Literary Question

Self-reflexivity or self-reference usually figures in what has become, even in ordinary journalism, the genre or canon of modernist work. At issue in a modernist work is the constituent language of an art form. Narrative structures, realist or figurative illusions, didactic purposes are eliminated or are subordinated to this issue. Art turns to its own basic means and materials; the artist's act or gesture is addressed to no one and has no other warrant or function than itself. In some such sense, modernist works are said to be self-questioning.

But the question is why it is significant to classify works in this way, and in what sense the classification answers to a period or a culture, more precisely, to *our* period of culture; in short in what sense they are *modern*. That, at any rate, was the question Foucault asked himself in the 1960s: "our task for today is to direct our attention to this nondiscursive language, this language which, for almost two centuries had stubbornly maintained its disruptive existence in our culture."[6] Foucault's answer starts with his first main thesis on modernism: modernist art (and particularly literature) is about the very essence or source of all art. "Writing, in our day, has moved infinitely closer to its source, to this disquieting sound which announces from the depths of language—once we attend to it—the source against which we take refuge and towards which we address ourselves."[7] Self-reflexivity in modernist work is a way in which art moves closer to its sources and its essence. Modernist writing is an attempt to "reapprehend the essence of literature in the movement that brought it into being."[8]

The central premise of the *nouvelle critique* is that modernist work *does* in fact discover the essence or the sources of art and literature. It is not that modernist works are the only ones to be self-reflexive or to be "meta-works," but that they are the ones whose task it is to reveal that such self-reflexivity is the essence of art. All art would be, as it were, ontological—not about the world or about the author, but about art itself, its origins, materials, and traditions. In modernism, art would in fact approach this "essence." As Roland Barthes put it in 1959, through its various forms from Flaubert to Robbe-Grillet, modernist writing is constantly asking itself the Oedipal question, "who am I?" It is like "that Racinian heroine who dies in knowing herself, but lives in searching for herself."[9]

The *nouvelle critique* was a *modernist* criticism in which avant-garde works were held to exemplify the essence of

all works, an essence which was then read back into the tradition. Hence it was assumed that all works tell of their own
creation, materials, traditions, and therefore of themselves. In
each literary work there is thus an "allegory of reading," a
secret reflection on the nature of language and of literature, a
hidden self-interpretation which ties the work to the whole
fabric of the literary tradition, and which criticism must ferret
out. Since every work is about language and literature, since
art is about itself, the laborious traditional practice of restating
it, or its "meaning," in some other nonliterary metalanguage
loses its point, and in fact is held to be impossible in principle.
Hence it appears that the "*ancienne critique*" labored under a
premodernist conception of the literary tradition as being a
sum of œuvres, their authors, and their meanings. In modernist
art and writing, tradition presents itself instead as an endless
fabric of interlocking references, a great reserve of materials
from which it draws without the obligation to represent or
express anything. Criticism can no longer remain a secondary
language which accredits and interprets individual works in the
primary language. It, too, must take the modernist turn, and
invent a new style, neither critical nor literary, but "paraliterary."[10] Current developments in this sort of thinking have
become so labyrinthine that it is useful to recall the modernist
impulse behind the *nouvelle critique:* the aim was to underwrite
modernist writing.

In the 1960s Foucault practiced his own version of
the *nouvelle critique*. In each work he uncovered a reference to
the particular artistic tradition in which the work figured, and
thus presented it as the self-referring instance of that tradition.
Las Meninas is a painting about painting in the tradition of
"illusionist space"; *Don Quixote* is the knight's tale which pa-
rodically retells all the previous knight's tales. *Justine* is the
conte in which all the moralist *contes* of the eighteenth century
are inverted. Even the defensive *Dialogues* of Rousseau are presented as a "language attempting in vain to call language
forth."[11]

More ambitiously, Foucault tried to construct a
"formal ontology of literature"[12]—an inventory of the various

forms or mirrors through which works had referred to themselves, their traditions, and their mediums. For every form there corresponded a way of identifying the work of art and a principle by means of which works were disseminated. Selecting works from European literature and painting, Foucault sketched the tale of a quest in which art, through many exploits, at last arrives at the "fatal space" in which it discovers its "source" and turns in on itself.

Foucault's history divides into three periods. There is an epic period, which, like the Renaissance hermeticism in the *Order of Things,* serves primarily as a defamiliarizing contrast for what follows. An epic refers to itself or its own creation by reference to the Gods who desire, or who observe the spectacle it recounts. Artists remain anonymous; divinity is what makes what is not yet called "art" possible. Then there is the classical period. Language is subordinated to "discourse," to representing the world through the rule-governed concatenation of signs. Hence it is a period of preciosity, rhetoric, and style—ways of figuratively reproducing what language is taken to represent. In his *Raymond Roussel,* Foucault describes the classical conception of style as "under the sovereign necessity of the words used, the possibility, at once indicated and masked, of saying the same thing, but in another way." (By contrast, "all Roussel's language, style inverted, seeks to say surreptitiously two things with the same words.")[13] In the classical age, authorship becomes central to the "authenticity" of a work, and writers incur the obligation to become "authors"—to discover the style, voice, or distinctive repertoire that genius creates and others must imitate. The classical era is the era of "classics"—works that embody the organistic form or "inner purposiveness" that genius engenders and connoisseurship rediscovers. It is the era of the universality and objectivity of taste, of "sensibility" as a correlate of art, and thus of the basic and uplifting humanity in the aesthetic experience.

There follows the modernist period in which "literature acquires an autonomous existence . . . by forming a sort of 'counter-discourse.'" "It breaks with the whole definition of *genres* as forms adapted to an order of representations, and becomes merely a manifestation of a language which has no other law than that of affirming . . . its own precipitous existence."[14] (Foucault suggests this parallel: the movement from Manet to Cézanne and on to Pollock by which painting affirms its own precipitous existence by forming a counter-illusionist space.)[15] In the modernist age, the languages of art are no longer tied down by "discourse" or the obligation to depict or express something. To write is no longer to express some inner urge or will, or to represent the society of one's time. It is to link books to other books, words to other words, in some endless library.

> The space of language today is not defined by Rhetoric but by the Library, but the ranging to infinity of fragmentary languages substituting for the double chain of Rhetoric the simple, continuous, and monotonous line of language left to its own devices, a language fated to be infinite because it can no longer support itself upon the speech of infinity.[16]

Modernism is not an era of the œuvre, the critic, and the genius, but of the archive, and the universal dissemination of all works (past and present). Its great emblem is the museum without walls: ". . . there is nothing for it to do but to curve back in a perpetual return upon itself as if its discourse could have no other content than the expression of its form."[17]

The epic period is a period of glorification and immortalization of heroes and their exploits, of the founding myth of peoples, and of stories without authors told and retold. The classical period is a period that gives rise to the values of "taste, pleasure, naturalness, truth." It is the period of the beaux arts, of "*Schöner Schein,*" a cultivated public and universalist "sensibilities." In the modernist period these classical values are overturned, and "the scandalous, the ugly, the impossible" become the object of an almost religious quest.[18] Literature discovers death, anxiety, and nameless desire as the limits and truth of experience. It is no longer an art of glorifying heroes or pleasing the senses. It is an art of transgression.

When art is stripped of any transcendent or aesthetic purpose, there remains only the bare artistic act. It looks into itself, it surrounds itself with a new madness only psychoanalysis can analyze. Foucault says transgression is the only *ethic* in modernism, for modernist culture can abide no morality.[19] Modernism is that culture that *requires* one to transgress in the "counter-discourse" of modern art.

The Modernist Sublime

The theme of transgression introduces Foucault's second main thesis on modernism—that the "source" or "essence" of art (and particularly of literature), the source that modernism finds or restlessly seeks (finds *by* restlessly seeking) is also the source or essence of experience, at least of *our* experience. The self-reflexivity of language in modern writing is a discovery of a "madness" in language; by purifying language of all obedience to "discourse," *écriture* articulates the "mad" source of experience, and so transcends or transgresses that which constitutes its limits. That "formless, mute, unsignifying region where language can find its freedom" is in fact just the same "region where death prowls, where thought is extinguished, where the promise of origin interminably recedes."[20]

One version of the second thesis is that modernist art "performs" something we believe we cannot represent in ordinary discourse—our own death, our object-less angst, our nameless desire, our fitful "eroticism." In the *Order of Things,* Foucault explains that we cannot represent such things to ourselves (or each other) since we take them to be the limits of what we *can* represent—they are our "finitudes," the limits of our experience. The transgression of modernist art is the only way we have to transcend them. Abstract art is not an abstract way of expressing feelings we might otherwise express or state to each other, but a way of "articulating" the very limits of our discourse. "To represent the unrepresentable" becomes the formula of an abstract or modernist *sublime.*[21]

The thesis of a modernist sublime is what connects the formal or formalist nature of modernist art to the great

figures of modernist contempt and condescension: the petit
bourgeois consumer of mass culture, the inauthentic *das Man*
with its "idle chatter," the "last man" of our flat, leveled-down
ascetic modern culture, the "neurotic" whose life is a long un-
successful denial of his perversion, anxiety, rage, and death.
Marx, Heidegger, Nietzsche, and Freud are thus the heroic
thinkers for this conception of modern experience, and, de-
pending on which master one prefers, one calls the unrepresentable or nondiscursive source of experience antibourgeois,
post-Cartesian, Dionysian, or pre-Oedipal. In short, the modernist sublime articulates the Dionysian wisdom that the world
of the inauthentic petit bourgeois neurotic rests on a fundamental Nothingness which he must deny; it defamiliarizes his
world, reverses its values, and points toward a new age. Of this
sublime transcendence, artists are the heroes. They articulate
"the abyss" which lies behind our world and the limits of what
we may experience in it. Artists no longer search for the pleasing style in which to "say the same things with other words,"
but heroically explore the very "source" of the language by
which we designate things, the source of the fatal uncanniness
(*Unheimlichkeit*) which nonartists know only at the cost of
madness. The modernist sublime is the sublimation of a modern madnesss, not because it creates a socially acceptable version of repressed contents, but because it articulates what is
uncivilizable and inarticulate about our desires—the source of
our particular kind of madness.

As critic of the entire post-Cartesian period, the era
of "representation" (*Vorstellung*) and of the *subjectum*,[22]
Heidegger is surely the central philosophical influence. In the
30s, notably through his reading of Hölderlin, we can trace a
movement in Heidegger's thought that goes from the postulation of angst as the fundamental experience (*Grunderfahrung*)
to art or *Dichtung* as the privileged way in which it is articulated for us. In the process we find the reaction against the
uprootedness of the modern subject, against the "essence" of
technology, against mass culture, ultimately against the "gigan-
tism" of America: we find also the dark prophecies of a new
mutation, a new and more *dichterisch* style of thought, and, of

course, a new god. Angst discloses the abysslike origins of our existence and that, in the end, is the "origin of the work of art." In *What Is Metaphysics?* (1929), Heidegger asserts that our uncanny relation to Being is shown to us in angst. Angst obsesses and oppresses our Being-there since beyond anything we can say it defamilarizes all-that-is, and confronts us with the Nothing behind all the familiar "things" in our world. Angst is therefore the condition for the disclosure of what-is to Man, the possibility of a transcendence of the *Da* of *Dasein,* of our limits or our finitude. Gradually one then discovers that the privileged mode in which to reveal and conceal this fundamental angst which silences us is precisely the work of art.[23]

Foucault's research into madness provided him, in the 1960s, with a historical perspective on this modern conception of the relation between art and experience—on the modernist sublime. In modernist writing, madness was being depsychiatrized or de-medicalized and returned to its source in "not the meaning nor the verbal material, but in the *play*" of language—in "this obscure and central liberation of speech from within the heart of itself, its uncontrollable fleeing towards a foyer ever without light"[24] The result was an interconnection between poetry and madness (and hence art and experience), subterranean and internal, unlike the platonic ecstasy which "protects (the poet) from illusion and exposes him to the radiant light of the gods."[25] It was also unlike the fool who represented the mad truth of resemblances in the classical age, when language was reduced to being the neutral and transparent vehicle of discourse.

Foucault was engaged in a long examination of how psychiatry had been able to present madness as an illness. He became interested in the fact that, starting in the nineteenth century, poets, writers, and philosophers numbered among its patients. Hölderlin, Nietzsche, Nerval, Artaud, Pound, and many others underwent episodes during which psychiatrists attempted unsuccessfully to treat them. When the modern artist is not mad, he fears he might be. In *How I Wrote Certain of My Books,* Raymond Roussel even republished Pierre Janet's case study of his illness, *De l'angoisse à l'extase.* In the madness of modern poets, misunderstood by psychiatry, Foucault discerned a new relation to the very language of poetry, and he speculated that this relation might survive the whole history of the psychiatrization of madness.

> Hence also this strange intimacy between madness and literature to which one should not lend the meaning of a psychological relation finally revealed. Uncovered like a language silencing itself and superimposing itself on itself, madness doesn't manifest or recount the birth of an œuvre (or something which, with genius or luck, could have become an œuvre); it designates the empty form whence the œuvre derives, that is to say the place from which it never ceases to be absent, where one will never find it because it was never there. In that pale region, this essential hiding, the common incompatibility of the œuvre and madness reveals itself; it is the blind spot of their possibilities and their mutual exclusion.[26]

Hence the centrality of Freud. Not that he provided the therapeutic means to allow our madness to be expressed, but rather that he "returned words to their very source—to this white region of self-implication where nothing is said."[27]

Thus Foucault was drawn to Freud; more precisely, to the version of Freud that had been elaborated by Lacan—psychoanalysis understood in terms of nineteenth-century literature, not nineteenth-century biology; understood not as a psychology of artists or the characters they create in fiction, but as a theory of the "being" of literature and its relation to the subject. With Lacan, psychoanalysis became a theory of what the "subject" must be if the claims of modernist literature to find a fundamental source of both experience and art were to be taken seriously. Psychoanalysis becomes the theory of the modernist sublime. In the famous *Rome Discourse* (1953), Lacan in fact offers a definition of psychosis as "language without discourse" which Foucault, ten years later, was to make the central terms of his definition of modernist writing.

In fact, in the 1930s, when Heidegger, reading Hölderlin, was lecturing on the essence of art, and Janet was calling his patient Roussel a *"pauvre fou,"* Lacan was arguing that a revolution in psychiatry would follow from a detailed linguistic study of the *écrits* of the mad.[28] His thesis studies a

woman who took dictations from voices, the results of which
were published by Eluard under the title *"poésie involontaire."*
Against Janet's theory of *la fonction du réel,* he argued that
auditory hallucination, as in the case of his patient, far from
being a failure of aural perception, was in fact a cataclysmic
alteration in the relation of the subject to her own speech, the
suppression of which in normal subjects enabled the "perception of the real" in the first place. In Lacan's work from the
1930s we may now read the ingredients of the transformation
of psychoanalysis into a practice that matches modernist poetic
experience: from the "automatism" of language he discovers in
psychosis comes the germ of the idea that the unconscious is
not a reservoir of repressed contents but is "structured like a
language." In psychosis he finds the fundamental alienation
constitutive of our experience he was shortly to analyze by
postulating a "mirror stage"; there is already an insistence that
an expressive or cathartic model of therapy (resembling a premodern poetry) be replaced by one in which the patient's
"language" speaks a truth which he must try to reconstitute in
his "concrete discourse"; there is also the notion that this
"language" must be understood in literary or rhetorical categories as a sort of hermetic writing and there is a startling connection between the movement away from discourse toward a mad
language and a feminization of the subject or a rediscovery of a
relation to the Mother. Finally there is Lacan's sense, typical of
literary modernism, that a technocratic normalizing psycho-
therapy, symbolized by America, is the source of the betrayal of
psychoanalysis as literary science, a theory of *la lettre.*

　　　All of these elements are brought together in
Lacan's interpretation of Judge Schreber's memoir that appears
in his summary of the Seminar on psychosis of 1955–56, in
which he introduced his claim that the origin of psychosis is a
"foreclosure of the paternal metaphor."[29] The memoir helps to
understand psychosis since it is self-reflexive: it is the delirious
account of how it becomes necessary and possible to write such
a work; its topic is "how I wrote this book" and is thus the
memoir of modern madness. Lacan sees the powers of creation
which Schreber attributed to divine rays (which Freud saw as

allegorical of libidinal flows) as an allegory of words or linguistic expressions; he takes the delirious theory of Creation as a theory of writing, and analyzes the hermetic *Grundsprache* as a transgressive linguistic play. And contra Freud, Lacan takes Schreber's feminization not as the result of suppressed homosexuality, but as a consequence of his delirious return to the sources of language.

In 1961, Laplanche then applied Lacan's theory of psychosis to *Hölderlin,* and, in 1962, Foucault reviewed his book (in 1965, Derrida reviewed Foucault's review).[30] Foucault argues that Hölderlin exemplifies a great cultural alteration in the relations between art and life, which Laplanche's style of criticism allows us to understand.

On the one hand, criticism, freeing Hölderlin from "the accumulated weight of a half-century of interpretations inspired by the disciplines of Stephan George," had discovered that it was "necessary to recapture [Hölderlin's] language at its source" namely at the "profoundly embedded point where poetry self-consciously discovers itself on the basis of its proper language." To understand that source we need to reformulate our views on the relation between life and art; a new cultural configuration is required to explain how it is that the "mute forms of madness" are linked "to the most essential aspects of a poem." We must ask "what *source* gives rise to the possibility of language."[31]

The answer, of course, is transgression, the secret of the modernist sublime. The heroism of the author is brought about with the decline of the epic, and "the psychological dimension in our culture is the negation of epic perception." Modernism, however, pushes the development of literature beyond this dimension, since it discovers that the limits of an œuvre are in fact the limits of psychological experience:

> The dissolution of a work in madness, this void to which poetic speech is drawn as to its self-destruction is what authorizes the text of a language common to both. These are not abstractions, but historical relationships which our culture must eventually examine if it hopes to find itself.[32]

A Post-Enlightenment Culture

That "our culture should find itself in these "histor-ical relationships" is precisely what Foucault himself was trying to work out in this period, and *The Order of Things* is his most sustained attempt to do so—to show that "literature in our day . . . is a phenomenon whose necessity has its roots in a vast configuration in which the whole structure of our thought and our knowledge is traced." This book elaborates Foucault's third main thesis on modernism: the culture in which art is free to take itself as an object in the sublime transgression of the limits of experience is the culture whose "fundamental problems" are "intimately linked" with the "question of the being of language."[33]

Literature had not been central to European cul-ture. In fact, Foucault asserts that since the sixteenth century it had been "foreign," denied, "overlain." In our period, however, it becomes "more and more that which must be thought."[34] *The Order of Things* is the story of the "return of language" which explains the central position of literature in our culture. Ours is a period in which language is taken to be at the root of all thought, and this is what "necessitates" modernist writing. It is not

a narcissism occurring within a literature freeing itself at last from what it has to say in order to speak henceforth only about the fact that it is language stripped naked. It is, in fact, the strict unfolding of Western culture in accordance with the necessity it imposed upon itself at the beginning of the nineteenth century.[35]

Contained in this thesis is another one: that our period, focused on language, gives rise to a post-Enlighten-ment literary culture. Following Kant, "The Enlightenment" usually refers to that period that considers science to be univer-sal and autonomous, art to be a matter of objective judgments of taste, and morals to consist in the self-legislation of universal laws by autonomous individuals—all three spheres having their foundations in the nature of Man. By contrast, in *The Order of Things,* Foucault paints a picture of modernist culture in which there is no "nature of man," science is no longer autonomous or universal, no morality is possible at all, and the task of articulating the "limits" of experience has fallen to avant-garde writing and art. All scientific, aesthetic, and moral problems are reduced to problems of language, and languages have no warrant or foundation beyond themselves. Thought is always attempting to change us by discovering the tacit language games constitutive of our "forms of life," by demystifying the hidden ideologies of our society or the unconscious structures of our experience. It tries "to think the unthought" (*penser l'impensé*).[36] Language becomes the limits of our being. It is only in transgressive writing that these limits are transcended; writers are the heroes of our age. This is a picture of what I call "post-Enlightenment literary culture."

This picture is built into the very structure of *The Order of Things* and determines the plot of the story it tells. As is often the case,[37] the figure referred to as "we" traces a circle of interpretation. The book is written from "our" modernist perspective, but also tells the story of how our perspective "necessarily" emerged. Thus, not only is "the question of the being of language . . . intimately linked with the fundamental problems of our culture,"[38] but what *we* take to be deep, fundamental, or "archaeological" in each previous era is found in *its* conception of language. In the preface, Foucault asserts that he ends "on the threshold of a modernity that we have not yet left behind" (p. xxiv); after the threshold it becomes possible for us to look back, in a burst of Borgesian laughter, on the preceding era and the "humanisms" that grew out of it. From this post-Enlightenment perspective, "we" then appear at the end of each chapter to review the "deep" arrangements of some earlier period, pointing in each case toward the *écriture* in our own times. It is thus we literary modernists who tell the story of how language has returned as the fundamental problem of our period, and our literary culture which thus "finds itself" by telling itself its own history.

The plot of the story is complicated by the fact that Foucault superimposes his history of literature in three periods (epic, classic, modern), with Cervantes, Sade, and company as heroes, on a highly original history of science—the history of an abrupt change that occurs concurrently in the study of life, labor, and language during the period from the French Revolution to Napoleon. The dual plot suggests a curious set of relations between literature and knowledge.

Later Foucault explains that by the "épistémè" of an age he meant not a world view or ideology but a system of possible discourse which underlies a body of knowledge and determines which groups of statements are susceptible of being true or false.[39] It would not seem, however, that he means to include painting and literature under this definition, since they are not really a part of such *savoirs;* on the contrary, modernist writing in particular is often thought to be, in the phrase of Georges Bataille, a *non-savoir.* Foucault's claims, such as "literature in our day . . . is a phenomenon whose necessity has its roots in a vast configuration in which the whole structure of our thought and our knowledge is traced," apparently mean not so much that literature occurs *within* that configuration as that it articulates its limits, and, in this sense, is *about* it as a whole. This in fact seems to be the general link between Foucault's two histories, the history of knowledge and the history of literature and painting. Arts are meta-epistemic, allegories of the deep arrangements that make knowledge possible. Thus, rather curiously, *Las Meninas* is about an order that underlies the seventeenth-century discussion of wealth, the Marquis de Sade is exploring the limits of the Port-Royal grammarians, and Raymond Roussel is discovering the "conditions of possibility of all knowledge about man."[40]

While Foucault rejects the traditional (Enlightenment) idea of progress in science and instead constructs his history of knowledge around sharp discontinuities, his literary history contains a hidden teleology. In periods of "break" or "rupture" (as in our period) literature and painting articulate or relate the "discontinuous" configurations, until in the modern period they asssume their "avant-garde" role. "Our" perspective obviously determines the literary story. It is not all a history of "influence." Nothing about the influence of Sade, the readings of his works, or their "effective history," prepares one for the view that they were about the limits of the épistémè of representation. Only *we* can see that a period of "counter-discourse" is initiated in his covert demonstration that desire cannot be captured in the rules of representation characteristic of knowledge in this era.

> Sade attains the end of classical discourse and thought . . . After him, violence, life and death, desire and sexuality will extend, below the level of representation, an immense expanse of shade which *we* are now attempting to recover, as far as *we* can, in *our* discourse, in *our* freedom, in *our* thought.[41]

And yet it is this progressive literary story that stands behind the story of the "return of language." It is the affinities between modernist literature and the hermetic tradition (for example, Mallarmé and Paracelsus) that make it plausible to see in "our" interest in language a return to the Renaissance hermeticism, when it was thought there was a language of the "signatures of things." Our literary discourse, freedom, thought, etc., determine that it is the Renaissance from which language "returns."

Foucault notes that in the late nineteenth century discussion of language goes off in many directions, a "dispersion" quite unlike what happens to the discussion of life and labor to which it had been previously epistemically linked.

> For philologists, words are like so many objects formed and deposited by history; for those who wish to achieve a formalization, language must strip itself of its concrete content and leave nothing visible but those forms of discourse that are universally valid; if one's intent is to interpret, then words become a text to be broken down so as to allow that other meaning hidden in them to emerge and become clearly visible; lastly, language may sometimes arise for its own sake in an act of writing that designates nothing other than itself.[42]

Interpretation and formalization are the two main tendencies; Freud and Russell being on either end of the "fork" that branches in those two directions. Interpretation includes the turn to the *nouvelle critique* (which "does not proceed from the observation that there is language towards the discovery of

what that language means, but from the deployment of mani-
fest discourse towards a revelation of language in its crude
being"). But the "most important" is the last development, in
which, this "being" itself is the issue: "the appearance of literature, of literature as such . . . [which] can possess neither
sound nor interlocutor, where it has nothing to say but itself,
nothing to do but shine in the brightness of its being."[43]

    Écriture is more important than the other paths lan-
guage takes in the "arrangement" of our period (*Finnegan's
Wake* would be more important for thought than the invention
of the predicate calculus) because it continues the "counter-
discourse" begun by Sade, and because it shares with modern
madness an experience of our limits; it was characteristic of the
classical period to repress or exclude such madness or counter-
discourse. Thus *écriture* announces a leap (*Ursprung,* origin)[44]
toward a new form of thought:

> The dispersion of language is linked, in fact, in a fundamental way
> with the archeological event we may designate as the disappearance
> of Discourse. To discover the vast play of language contained once
> more within a single space might be just as decisive a leap towards a
> wholly new form of thought as to draw to a close a mode of know-
> ing constituted during the previous century.[45] The threshold be-
> tween Classicism and modernity . . . had been definitively crossed
> when words ceased to intersect with representations and to provide
> a spontaneous grid for the knowledge of things. At the beginning of
> the nineteenth century, they rediscovered their ancient enigmatic
> density. . . .[46]

Thus we return to "our" assumption in the preface that *écriture*
is what the classical period had to cover over. Normally some
version of "disenchantment" is used to describe the emergence
of the classical era—an end to prejudice, magic, and superstition. But for Foucault that is only the consequence of a shift in
the relations between "words and things" which modernism
would again reverse. Cervantes and the Spanish Baroque
rather than Descartes (who contributes to the repression of
madness) initiate the "fundamental arrangement" of the period, shown in the attitude toward language (and, therefore,
toward literature).

Thus, "one might say, if one's mind is filled with ready-made concepts, that the seventeenth century marks the disappearance of the old superstitious or magical beliefs and the entry of nature at long last into the scientific order but what we must grasp and attempt to reconstitute are the modifications that affected knowledge itself at the archaic level." On the "archaic level," the central fact is rather that "language (withdrew) from the midst of beings themselves and . . . entered a period of transparency and neutrality."[47] On the deep level, neither a discovery of correct methods or a new paradigm (neither "rationalism" nor "mechanism") made it possible for there to exist interpretation-proof regularities the rational subject might discover. Rather, symbolized in the baroque ironies about the end of the world of resemblances, what made such surface phenomena as rationalism and mechanism possible was a reduction of language to a transparent medium for the ideas or discourse through which a subject might represent the world. It is, of course, in modernism that this basic assumption "disappears," in the age of the return of language in which literature attains the limits of subjective experience, a counter-discourse, a new madness.

In short, while in our age literature is "more and more what must be thought," the "fundamental arrangement" of the Enlightenment period it replaces was precisely that *our* literature was *unthinkable* for it, hence "foreign," "covered over," and so on. In our post-Enlightenment culture, the whole self-conception of the Enlightenment as rooted in a basic nature of Man is only a surface whose depth is incompatible with "transgressive writing." Hence, for us, "Man had been a figure occurring between two modes of language; or, rather, he was constituted only when language, having been situated within representation, and, as it were, dissolved in it, freed itself from that situation at the cost of its own fragmentation."[48] Just what Foucault was to denounce about the 1960s literary theory is contained in this thesis of a post-Enlightenment literary culture, which figured so crucially in his preoccupations in *The Order of Things:* "we" should no longer find ourselves in such a culture, but rather in more "specific" political struggles; writing should no longer be a "focus of things," something that "must be thought."

He reverses the central premise of his own work: the "fundamental arrangements" in our history are not about language but about power. It is misguided to formulate the problem of knowledge as a problem of language (translation, terminology, pragmatics) as though a study of language could shed much light on the workings of knowledge, particularly knowledge about ourselves in such disciplines as psychiatry or criminology. Hence there is little basis for the view that art or literature is meta-epistemic, or that the Enlightenment was basically only an understanding of language that represses writing. The questions of the Enlightenment, therefore, return. Morals become an issue within the new politics of specific intellectuals (nuclear weapons—Oppenheimer, "the environment," genetics, but also medicine, psychiatry, criminology— the moral questions about what enables knowledge to become an instrument of policies). A study of language and literature is of little use in understanding this basic problem of our knowledge. Even in thought, language, far from introducing a new form, loses its centrality. Hence Foucault's sense that, far from being the cock's crow of a new age, it is the swan song of the obsessions of an old one.

With the centrality of language for contemporary thought goes the whole historical rationale for an "avant-garde" of writing. That modernist writing finds in itself the sources of all art, that all previous work is but an allegorical anticipation of it, that it articulates some mad, sublime, ineffable basis of experience, that it augurs a whole new mode for thought—all this "theorization about writing" is then the wrong path for specific intellectuals to follow.

Foucault's Autobiography

Foucault's condemnation of 1960s literary theory is thus autobiographical. It is a rejection of his own preoccupations with modernism in the period, and even of his own "literary" style.

Formalism is one name *The Order of Things* uses for this attitude—"this general indication of our experience, which may be termed 'formalism.'"[49] *Formalism* is a term for the assumptions through which the "disruptions" and "transgressions" of the "counter-discourse" of modernist art were misunderstood and overestimated.

The problems Foucault finds in formalism, however, do not require a return to a precritical realism or figuration, or a renewed historicism. We may still recognize that there is (and for the last hundred years has been), in our art, a politics of forms—of the procedures, techniques, truth claims, principles of authorship, and dissemination. But that politics is not (and was not) a politics *of* the forms as such, as the "source" or "essence" of all art or literature, as the triumph of pure self-examination, or as a struggle, against all forms of "representation," to attain a Dionysian wisdom about their limits. The problem with formalism is not that it draws attention to forms, but that its understanding of the politics of forms is *unspecific*—it cannot identify the specific struggles in which the forms figure. That is why Foucault's praise of "specific intellectuals" entails a reversal in the three theses on modernism I have isolated in his early writing.

Against the first thesis, it is wrong to locate the *essence* of art in its capacity to take itself as object. As a principle of criticism, self-reflexivity (the view that all arts have always been about themselves, their languages, and their traditions) commits one in the end to a misleading *internal* conception of tradition, to a "literary" conception of literature. In modernity, it leads one to a politics of the supremacy of the literary and of the writer rather than to a politics of the specific ways in which works participate or have participated in concrete struggles. Against his second thesis on modernism, Foucault now seems to hold that the opposition between a "literary" or "poetic" madness and a psychiatric "illness," and thus of the notion that Freud moves us from the second to the first, rests on a misguided contrast between literary and scientific or technocratic ways of representing ourselves. His central concern now is with a "technology of the self" which is found in literature—an unthinkable project for his earlier position. He attempts not to determine what escapes the limits of representation or of experience, but to specify *how* the terrible figures of the modernist sublime, death, desire, and anxiety, have been put into words. Literature has no privilege in this, and it would thus be misguided to see in literature as such the main source of opposition to the power of "normalization" in our society.

These objections are contained in the problem with Foucault's third thesis on modernism: the problem with the very concept of modernity and with its implied reference to those of us who use the concept. For *modern* is a deictic term, as Foucault himself observes at one point in *The Order of Things;* a contrast "between *our* prehistory and what is still contemporary" should replace the contrast between classical and modern. In Foucault's later writing we can see how this idea is elaborated. *Modernity* comes to refer to what in the past is still operative in *our* present. *Discipline and Punish* purports to be a "genealogy of modern morals" and a "history of the present." The implied deictic reference is to "specific intellectuals" and not to avant-garde or vanguard intellectuals. For Foucault takes the "present" to refer to entities like "mental illness" or "the criminal personality," which are presupposed by our current practices and, in ways we don't realize, are rooted in the past (see next chapter). To write a history of the present is thus to draw attention to the constitution of those objects, and its consequences, and thus to open up our "modernity" to change. No attempt is made to predetermine what this change will be; we are committed to no general scheme of transformation and no single alternative. Hence, we no longer claim an avant-garde or vanguard relation to our own modernity, nor do we claim to announce a whole new form of thought and society. Conversely, the problem with taking art as allegorical of an age, as Foucault did in *The Order of Things*, is that it entails that there is a reality (or "spirit") of an age as a whole, which precedes our specific problems and which we as "universal" intellectuals have the special office of articulating or representing. That is how we arrive at the avant-gardist view that sees art as standing on the "threshold" or the point of "rupture" in our age, and thus, independently of the specific issues of our situation, we end up believing that Artaud may announce the end to the institution of psychiatry, or Mallarmé the institution of authorship.

In fact, the "individualization of the author" belongs to a broader or "deeper" politics which involves many other procedures to individualize us, including, for example, the individualization of homosexuals. Just as literature circulated for years without the idea that it belongs to an author whose intentions it must express, and thus, without the obligation to *be* an author, for centuries homosexual *acts* circulated without there arising the idea that they are the expression of the homosexual kind of *person*, and thus without the obligation to decide whether or not one *is* such a person. These two procedures to "individualize" intersect in the "political reality" of the homosexual writer—a matter of obviously specific concern for Foucault.[50] To examine *how* specifically the individuality of both author and homosexual were constituted and then combined in our times (an examination that might well include a discussion of the forms as well as the themes of our literature and art) illustrates Foucault's approach to "specific" problems in our modernity. The point of such an examination would not be to place oneself, or the literature one examines, in an avant-garde position in relation to our whole society or culture, but to increase our freedom with respect to a specific way in which we are determined. Not only does the third thesis on modernism make the formalist assumption that "basic languages" are what is at issue in our art, but that thesis also rests on an unspecific "literary" conception of our position in modern culture.

Foucault's own attempt to offer a specific analysis of literature and art in modernity has in fact centered on this issue of individuality and subjectivity—on the politics of the terms and categories by which we identify ourselves and each other, and on the history of how we have been "constituted as subjects in both senses." Drawing on a preoccupation in recent French historiography, he treats literature or art not as a tradition of great works nor as a group of texts referring to one another in the infinite web of intertextuality, but as *documents* through which are constituted central categories of individuality in our modern life. He does not revert to the preformalist image of the critic who comments on his world. He does not ask how works represent or reflect the societies of an age or resolve its fundamental contradictions. Rather he asks how, in their forms as well as in their topics, arts figure within a configuration of other kinds of documents to constitute a political reality. More precisely, he attempts to specify the documents and the politics that have made of our own subjective identities a central problem in our literature and art—project which the old thesis that the "subject is constituted in language" both suggested and obscured.

One might regard Foucault's more recent work as a complex political reelaboration of his 1960s theme that "the psychological dimension in our culture is the negation of epic perceptions." The psychological dimension in our art and literature would include not simply the institution of authorship, and the obligation of authors to ferret out and reveal their innermost secrets, but also a preoccupation with the ugly little details of ordinary life, an importance ascribed to familial relations and their disturbances, an obsession with the crime or deviance that may be lurking inside us, and the whole issue of *secrets* as metaphors of the human heart and of the incompleteness of self-knowledge. His central question is how. How has the "psychological dimension" been put into discourse and how has there arisen an obligation to turn inward to discover the truth? Foucault's hero is now not Sade but Diderot—specifically Diderot's *Les Bijoux indiscrets*, an erotic farce from the heart of the Enlightenment in which men in learned societies explain the power of the "sex" of women to speak, not knowing it has been incited by the magic ring of the Sultan (who represents the French monarch).

Discipline and Punish explores our modern psychologizing individualization in terms of "disciplines." Disciplines *are* individualizing classifications of populations (attention is given to each and every member of a population individually so as to enable individual prediction or intervention); they introduce our modern politics "to substitute for a power manifested through the brilliance of those who exercise it, a power that insidiously objectifies those on whom it is applied; to form a knowledge about these individuals rather than to deploy the ostentatious signs of sovereignty."[51] The transition from epic literature is part of this change in the "modality of power." Procedures such as commemorative rituals and glorifications of sovereignty are replaced by such documents as case studies, dossiers, and standardized examinations.[52] Instead of sanctifying heroes, the focus is on the internal sources of ordinary behavior and on its deviation from norms. Thus,

> if from the early Middle Ages to the present day the "adventure" is an account of individuality, the passage from the epic to the novel, from the noble deed to the secret singularity, from long exiles to the internal search for childhood, from combats to phantasies, it is also inscribed in the formation of a disciplinary society. The adventure of our childhood no longer finds expression in 'le bon petit Henri,' but in the misfortunes of "little Hans." The *Romance of the Rose* is written today by Mary Barnes; in the place of Lancelot, we have Judge Schreber.[53]

The History of Sexuality enlarges this analysis of how documents that focus on the exemplary deeds and laws of great men give way to documents that focus on the internal or secret desires of ordinary individuals. Confession, Foucault conjectures, is at the heart of it. There are the documents of avowal: "interrogations, consultations, autobiographical narratives, letters . . . recorded, transcribed, assembled into dossiers, published and commented on." Through them we move from an epic to a modern literature:

> We have passed from a pleasure to be recounted and heard, centering on the heroic or marvelous narration of "trials" of bravery or sainthood to a literature ordered according to the infinite task of extracting from the depths of oneself, in between the words, a truth which the very form of confession [*aveu*] holds out like a shimmering mirage.[54]

It is a change in forms (for example, in narrative structures), in topics (for example, in the stress on the details of ordinary life and on the family), in attitudes of reception (inwardness and "absorption") as well as in dissemination (printing, publishing, authorship, and so on). Sade is no longer the first to demonstrate that desire escapes represention in discourse, but, by "projecting the seventeenth-century pastoral into literature,"[55] he helps to constitute desire as something mysterious and internal that must be sought through meticulous procedures. Freud marks no departure or "rupture." There may be a similarity between literary or rhetorical forms and analytic techniques, and it may be true that both are concerned with the same kind of "truth" about ourselves. But it is just in this respect that both may be said to have roots in the same kinds of procedures of confession. *The Interpretation of Dreams* might stand as an emblem. It is, after all, an autobiography and a confession (since Freud's own dreams are at issue, even his dreams about the sacrifices he must make to science in analyzing his own dreams). Yet, in it, no attention is paid to dreams of actual sexual *acts* (as in premodern books on dream interpretation), while the secret truth of dreams is always to be found in those internalized deviant infantile sexual desires which only the laborious techniques of self-examination can uncover.

"Modern sexuality from Sade to Freud," Foucault wrote in the 1960s.[56] In the seventies this had become for him a sexuality not of transgression but of confession, not of "expenditure" but of coersive fixing of identities. Thus it would be rhapsodical or illusory to think that the "transgressions" of modernist writing were subverting all individualization. For individualization is not a "literary" matter of representation in language, but a complex political reality no linguistic play can dispel. This realization was an event in Foucault's own "autobiography," indeed, one that led him to see his theoretical work as autobiographical:

> Each time I have attempted to do theoretical work, it has been on the basis of elements from my experience—always in relation to processes that I saw taking place around me. It is in fact because I

thought I recognized something cracked, dully jarring, or disfunc-
tioning in things I saw, in the institutions with which I dealt, in my
relations with others, that I undertook a particular piece of work,
several fragments of an autobiography.[57]

Such "autobiography" is the reverse of self-expression or confession. It is an analysis of what in one's modernity (the processes going on around one) fixes one's identity, an analysis of
the modern politics of individualization.

The Ethic of Subjectivity

At the philosophical core of Foucault's embrace of
modernism was the fundamental question "what is language?"
and the disruption that question would have introduced into
our culture. His turn to the critic or writer as "specific intellectual" is his move away from a century-long obsession with
language. That is what dies in the swan song of literary theory.
Foucault preserves one idea: that the subject is constituted. But
he rejects the Lacanian thesis that the subject is constituted in
language. Our subjectivity is constituted through many different kinds of practice, only some of which are literary or linguistic, such as the practices of confession and or individualization.
The "author-function" belongs to a larger constellation of individualizing practice; the literary challenges to it belong to a
larger politics of subjectivity. We need an analysis of the nature
and limits of the practices through which our experience is
constituted. The writer and critic join a wider and less formalist
intellectual politics: the politics of the problematization of subjectivity as a challenge to a culture at once individualizing and
universalizing.

In *Writing Degree Zero,* Barthes had argued, against
the Sartrian conception of literature as engagement, that the
challenge to "bourgeois" morality and literary institutions in
early modernism resided in the formulation of an ethic of
language: that ethic would be continued in the practice of
écriture. The "ends of modernism" are found in the undoing of

this historical link between formalist experiment and the challenge to "bourgeois" institutions, between the ethic of language and its historical sources.

Foucault comes to deny that the nature of literature lies in the being of language, the nature of the artistic act in the relation to material or medium, the nature for culture in the web of intertextuality open to sovereign artistic play. As the subject is not constituted in language so the ethic of writing is not an ethic of language. Foucault advances a new ethic: not the ethic of transgression, but the ethic of constant disengagement from constituted forms of experience, of freeing oneself for the invention of new forms of life. Modernism is not so monolithic as it was once supposed. In its preformalist and postformalist moments, it touches on Foucault's conception of an ethic, not of objects and materials, but of subjective experience itself.

Thus we might shift our attention away from the Mallarméan focus on language back to the classical questions of early modernism, to Baudelaire's question in the "Painter of Modern Life": what form of life must be led for the question "what is language" to become the question of literature? Baudelaire proposes an ethic not yet of forms of art but of forms of life, an aesthetics of existence, not of objects.

The Baudelairian figures in the cosmopolitan city (the dandy, the flâneur) introduce this problem of an aesthetics of existence in a modern rather than epic form: not how to live so as to leave behind glorious memories, but how to use writing to invent forms of experience other than the ones previously prescribed. It introduces an ethic based neither in science nor religion nor in Kantian moral duties: an ethic that is a matter of choice of life rather than abstract obligation—the problem of writing becomes the aesthetics of self-invention.

Postformalist works like performance take up such Baudelairian questions in a new way: one's life, one's concrete body, one's photographable presence (as distinct from one's role in a representation) is incorporated into a work that attempts to disturb the general or constituted sense of self. The parodic, ironic, or "simulacral" repetition of words, situations, gestures, or images in experience induce a sense of their contingency. We do not need to take these figurations as natural; we may choose to live otherwise. In such works, "distance" is not a condition for artistic representation; it is a means in an ethic-aesthetic that holds we may invent other kinds of experience. It is thus an ethic for which freedom lies neither in self-discovery or authenticity nor in the "free-" play of language, but in a constant attempt at self-disengagement and self-invention.

This becomes Foucault's own ethic as a writer and intellectual. It is the direction his work takes with the ends of modernism. It is his way of continuing the modernist challenge to the constitution of the subject. It amounts to a particular historical and political stance which we may find in the active nominalism in Foucault's histories, in his politics of revolt, and in his transformation of critique. It is the ethic of subjectivity, the ethic of the ends of modernism.

Notes

1. Michel Foucault, "Truth and Power," in *Power/Knowledge*, p. 127. Similar denunciations are to be found in "Intellectuals and Power: A Conversation between Michel Foucault and Gilles Deleuze" (1972), in *Language, Counter-Memory, Practice*, p. 214; and *I, Pierre Rivière . . .* , tr. p. xi.

2. See Michel Foucault, "Georges Canguilhem: Philosopher of Error," *I & C*, no. 7, pp. 52–59.

3. Foucault, *Power/Knowledge*, p. 114.

4. "The function of the intellectual is to criticize bourgeois language under the very reign of the bourgeoisie." Roland Barthes, *La Grain de la voix* (Paris: Editions du Seuil, 1981), p. 187. For later hesitations on precisely what constitutes bourgeois language, see Barthes' interview with Bernard-Henri Lévy in the same volume, pp. 251ff.

5. Michel Foucault, *The Order of Things*, p. 306.

6. Foucault, *Language, Counter-Memory, Practice*, p. 39.

7. *Ibid.*, p. 60.

8. Foucault, *The Order of Things*, p. 300.

9. Roland Barthes, "Littérature et métalanguage," in *Essais critiques* (Paris: Editions du Seuil), 1964, p. 106.

10. See Rosalind Krauss, "Poststructuralism and the 'Paraliterary,'" *October* (Summer 1980), no. 13, pp. 36–40.

11. Michel Foucault, "Introduction," to Jean-Jacques Rousseau, *Dialogues* (Paris, A. Colin, 1962).

12. Foucault, *Language, Counter-Memory, Practice*, p. 59.

13. Michel Foucault, *Raymond Roussel*, p. 25.

14. Foucault, *The Order of Things*, p. 300.

15. "Flaubert is to the library what Manet is to the museum. They both produced works in a self-conscious relation to earlier paintings or texts— or rather to the aspect in painting or writing that remains indefinitely open. They erect their art within the archive." Foucault, *Language, Counter-Memory, Practice*, p. 92. The allusion is no doubt to André Malraux, whose *Le Musée imaginaire* appeared in 1965. Already in *Saturne* Malraux suggested that the mark of Manet's modernity was his making art itself the "unique object" of painting, a theme developed by Georges Bataille in his remarkable *Manet* (Paris: Skira, 1955). Bataille is, of course, author of the concept of transgression that Foucault develops.

16. Foucault, *Language, Counter-Memory, Practice*, p. 67.

17. Foucault, *The Order of Things*, p. 300.

18. *Ibid.*

19. Foucault, *Language, Counter-Memory, Practice*, pp. 35, 116; and *The Order of Things*, p. 328.

20. Foucault, *The Order of Things*, p. 383.

21. See Jean-François Lyotard, "Presenting the Unpresentable: The Sublime," *Artform* (April 1982), 20(8):64–69. Lyotard derives the idea of the beautiful/sublime distinction from Kant, but of course there is a complex history in which the distinction travels through Schiller, Schelling, and Hegel to Schopenhauer, who thought of the sublime as the Will contemplating itself. It is in this form that it was transmuted into Nietzsche's distinction between Apollonian and Dionysian. This latter is, in fact, the more immediate background for Lyotard. As far back as its Longinian origins, the sublime seems to refer to an epic nobility in an effete "aestheticized" (modern) culture; that was certainly the case in Boileau's preferences for *les anciens*. It is thus linked to Bataille's theme of sovereignty—the modernist sublime being the sublime not of the hero but of the artist.

22. Heidegger's characterization of modernity in "The Age of the World-Picture," in *The Question Concerning Technology* (New York, Harper and Row, 1979).

23. Philippe Lacoue-Labarthe connects the theme of the *unheimliche* origin of art with Heidegger's relation to Nazism. See "Transcendence Ends in Politics," *Social Research* (Summer 1982), 49(2):405–440; and *Les Fins de l'homme* (Paris, Editions Galilée, 1981).

24. Michel Foucault, "La Folie, l'absence d'oeuvre," *La Table Ronde* (1964), no. 196, p. 16.

25. Foucault, *Language, Counter-Memory, Practice*, p. 75.

26. Foucault, "La Folie, l'absence d'oeuvre," p. 19.

27. *Ibid.*, p. 18.

28. "Écrits 'inspirés': schizographie"; see also Jacques Lacan, "La

Problème du style," in *De la psychose paranoïaque* (Paris, Editions du Seuil, 1975).

29. Jacques Lacan, "On a Question Preliminary to Any Possible Treatment of Psychosis," in *Écrits/A Selection*, Alan Sheridan, tr. (New York: Norton, 1977), p. 199.

30. Michel Foucault, "Le 'non' du père," *Critique* (1962), no. 178, pp. 195–206; tr. in *Language, Counter-Memory, Practice*, pp. 68–86; Jean Laplanche, *Hölderlin et la question du père* (Paris, P.U.F., 1961); Jacques Derrida, "La Parole soufflée," in *L'Écriture et la différence* (Paris, Editions du Seuil, 1967).

31. Foucault, *Language, Counter-Memory, Practice*, pp. 68–69 and 71–72.

32. *Ibid.*, pp. 75, 85.

33. Foucault, *The Order of Things*, pp. 383, 302.

34. *Ibid.*, p. 44.

35. *Ibid.*, p. 384. This is obviously a weak or pejorative notion of narcissism. In her remarkable *Lecture du Narcisse* (Paris: Didier, 1982), Anne Boyman develops a deeper sort of connection between the narcissism in art and experience characteristic of modernism.

36. *Ibid.*, pp. 322–327.

37. Compare the role of the *für uns* in Hegel's *Phenomenology of Spirit*.

38. Foucault, *The Order of Things*, p. 382.

39. See Foucault, *Power/Knowledge*, pp. 112–113, where he says he had confused the episteme "too much with systematicity, theoretical form or something like a paradigm." On the contrast between paradigms and epistemes, see Ian Hacking, "Foucault's Immature Science," *Noûs* (1979), no. 13, pp. 39ff.

40. Foucault, *The Order of Things*, p. 375.

41. *Ibid.*, p. 211, emphasis added.

42. *Ibid.*, p. 304.

43. *Ibid.*, pp. 298, 300.

44. See Heidegger, *The Origin of the Work of Art* (New York, Harper and Row, 1971).

45. Foucault, *The Order of Things*, p. 307.

46. *Ibid.*, p. 304.

47. *Ibid.*, pp. 54, 56.

48. *Ibid.*, p. 386.

49. *Ibid.*, p. 384.

50. Conservative critic John Simon is a good case of someone who would "individualize" the homosexual writer. Having argued that male homosexuals are congenitally sick, infantile, and narcissistic and therefore have less "human potential" than others, Simon goes on to complain of their ubiquitous presence even in the audiences of artistic productions. See "Homosexuals in Life and Art," *The New Leader*, October 28, 1974. In a review of "avowed [*sic*] homosexual" Michel Foucault's *The History of Sexuality*, Simon claims that the book derives essentially from Foucault's identity as a "homosexual writer": "I

cannot claim more than cursory knowledge of the previous work of Foucault, who, like Roland Barthes, is a professor at the renowned and formidable Collège de France. But what I do know of his books on language, madness, hospitals and prisons . . . establishes this sociologist-philosopher-linguisticist [sic] . . . as a master of paradox." According to Simon's argument, paradox is also the province of Oscar Wilde and Jean Genet, whose works, he says, constitute "criminal-pederastic propaganda." "Paradox Lost," *The New Leader,* December 4, 1978. Foucault argues that there is such a thing as a homosexual identity in our art, but that it is not a result of an intrinsic sexual nature, but of a politics—a politics to which remarks such as Simon's, however unfounded and silly, necessarily contribute. For one account of Foucault's thoughts on the subject, see "Sexual Choice, Sexual Act: An Interview with Michel Foucault," *Salmagundi* (Fall 1982–Winter 1983), nos. 58–59, pp. 10–24.

51. Michel Foucault, *Discipline and Punish,* Alan Sheridan, tr. (New York, Pantheon Books, 1977), p. 220.

52. Foucault differs from the *Annales* historians in using documents not to make inferences about demographic trends or price cycles, for example, but about the ways they themselves constitute a political reality, in this case the power to individualize. In his classic defense of quantitative methodology in history ("L'Histoire quantitative," *Annales E. S. C.,* 1971, vol. 26, no. 1), François Furet notes in passing that there is such a politics in documentation, so that, for example, "the difference between the number of peasant uprisings under Henry II and Louis XIII may reflect first and foremost the progress of monarchical civilization." Foucault would conduct research into the administrative sources about uprisings in France not in order to reconstitute the uprisings themselves but to analyze the politics of dealing with them, and hence "the progress of monarchical civilization." On Foucault's divergence from the *Annales* historians, see Michelle Perrot, ed., *L'Impossible Prison* (Paris, Edition du Seuil, 1980); and the next chapter.

53. Foucault, *Discipline and Punish,* p. 193.

54. Michel Foucault, *The History of Sexuality* (New York, Vintage Books, 1978), pp. 73, 59.

55. *Ibid.,* p. 21.

56. Foucault, *Language, Counter-Memory, Practice,* p. 29.

57. Michel Foucault, "Est-il donc important de penser?" *Libération* (Paris), May 30–31, 1981.

CHAPTER TWO

The Politics of Revolt

Foucault's Dilemma

Foucault wrote histories in several areas and periods. He also wrote about the discipline of history and its methods. Typically, philosophers have paid attention primarily to his meta-history, while historians have ignored it, preferring to judge his work on their own terms. But there is a further complication. Like Sartre, Foucault was an "intellectual" with public positions, and as such, he had to worry about the political aims and consequences of both his histories and their methods. All three facets of his work are perhaps less internally consistent than anyone imagines; yet it is instructive to take them as a whole.

Foucault has often been seen as Sartre's philosophical rival. Yet as an intellectual he shares with Sartre an inclination to present his work as nonacademic and nonspecialized, and as addressed in a nontechnocratic way to basic issues in the lives of all of us. And like Sartre, as Foucault assumes this intellectual role, he moves from primarily epistemological to primarily political concerns, identified with an oppositional Left, though not with a Party, or with any claim to bureaucratic or charismatic authority. In 1972, Foucault made a point of agreeing with philosopher Gilles Deleuze that intellectuals should no longer see themselves as "representing the masses"; they should stand apart and offer useful analyses for specific struggles.

There is a cluster of problems common to both Foucault's history and his meta-history that poses a dilemma for his left intellectual commitment. The dilemma belongs to a more general situation of French intellectuals attributed variously to a devaluation of Marxist thought, to a decline in the oppositional spirit symbolized by 1968, an "end of ideology," or even to the Socialist victory, but with the result that it can no longer be taken for granted that an intellectual is automatically *de gauche*.

In his 1976 presentation of his history of sexuality, Foucault introduces one theme that might be read as a critical analysis of a left sensibility—his conjecture that most of our talk about sexual "liberation" and "revolution" in fact belongs to a circumscribed little practice which it is now important to reinterpret as continuing a long history of internalizing domination. His concluding words are that there is an irony in the historical constitution of what we think of as our sexuality: that we were ever led to believe that our liberation was at issue.

I will suggest that a more general philosophical problem about freedom is involved in this irony. It was, of course, precisely Sartre who attempted to make freedom into *the* philosophical problem. Foucault took exception. English readers of *The Order of Things* are told, for example, that "If there is one approach that I do reject, it is . . . the phenomenological one."[1] Foucault maintained that there exists no subject, empirical or transcendental, individual or collective, that is prior to and constitutive of history; he thought that the circumstance that philosophers sought to determine the constitutive categories of our "life-world" might itself be analyzed in terms of historical bodies of discourse tacitly governed by anonymous rules. Hence, there is an inclination to assimilate Foucault to the later Heidegger as against Sartre—to Heidegger's "anti-humanist" understanding of freedom, not as will or as a fundamental choice as to who or what we are, but as the freeing or "clearing" of the possibilities of an age (see following chapter).

The problem is that, as an intellectual, Foucault obviously had much more in common with Sartre than with Heidegger. He worried much more about concrete demands in French prison riots or about the rather "existential" opposition of East European dissidents, than about anything like the Destiny of the German People. His intellectual stance was not primarily about our relation to a tradition of learning. He had none of Heidegger's talk of a People identified with a national philosophical language; his analysis of localized bits of "discourse" paid almost no attention to the issue of national languages. Moreover, his contributions to the politics of prisoners, mental patients, or homosexuals would seem to require *some* conception of a *political* freedom, as would his more general attempt to advance a "philosophy of power." And yet it is not clear how such political freedom would be squared with Heidegger's idea of the "Clearing" of an age.

For such reasons, it is instructive to consider more closely what it is about Foucault's meta-historical stance, or his actual historical works, that determines ambiguities with respect to his left intellectual commitments.

The meta-historical dilemma

Meta-historically, Foucault's commitment to a nonvoluntaristic, nonhumanistic freedom within history involves him in a dilemma about historical *change*. According to his early thesis of radical discontinuities in history, change, while nondeliberate, is nevertheless not caused or necessitated either by internal contradiction or by external forces. Thus the assertion of discontinuity may be read as positing a freedom by which new systems of possibility are opened up, or "cleared," and as defending this freedom from misleading and apocryphal attributions of continuities of progress, or "dialectical" transformation.

Histoire de la folie introduces the term "archaeology" for the sort of analysis through which such discontinuous "strata" are uncovered or "excavated." In *The Order of Things*, the metaphor is used to cover the assumption that there exist regularities in our "informal knowledge" which determine systems of possible discourse—what counts as relevant data or evidence, what kinds of objects are discussed, what kinds of sentences are capable of being true or false. The regularities are tacit. They are not explicit commitments, and cannot be held as a consistent whole by anyone. On the "deep" level, there are no heroes, and discourse is anonymous. Therefore the change from one such system of possibility to another cannot be the result of an awareness of internal difficulties, or of some collective decision or action. Some historical changes may be in some ways deliberate. But, on the archaeological level, where *kinds* of deliberate choices are determined, change is not decided upon. In particular an archaeological regularity is not maintained by misguided views or by mystified assent; in this sense it is unlike an ideology: it is not maintained *because* it is ideologically functional. For these reasons, deep historical regularity is nonnecessary, though deep historical change is nondeliberate.

How much of our informal knowledge in fact conforms to the pattern of discontinuous change can be debated. But there is also this dilemma: even if we grant discontinuity and agree that deep or archeological change is nondeliberate and nonnecessitated, what are we to do when confronted with "deep regularities" in our current situation to which we are opposed? Are we not reduced either to resigning ourselves to them or to hoping for some apocalyptic change? If no one else is free to bring about deep change, then how can we be?

There are many indications that, at least as an intellectual, Foucault *was* strongly opposed to much of what he found in our "deep" history. He was deeply, *archaeologically,* opposed to the "enlightened" or technocratic ways our civilization has devised for dealing with insanity, sickness, crime, and sexuality. Indeed the term "archaeology" is first used in *Histoire de la folie* to describe an excavation of forces that had "silenced" a cultural celebration of madness Foucault admired, through the emergence of institutions of mental health he did not. Similarly, even in *The Order of Things,* it is clear that Foucault is hostile to the culture that reifies Man, and urges the reader to embrace the post-humanist age he foresees. By contrast, for example, the change from the "prose of the world" (Renaissance hermeticism) to the "order of representation" (classical thought) is described in neutral terms, though it is archaeologically no different than the one Foucault prophesies.

On the one hand, change thus risks becoming *so* deep that it remains beyond the reach of any reform or even revolution, and, on the other hand, the point of the analysis, inasmuch as it is not merely antiquarian is to offer criticism and to help bring about some such deep change. In short, Foucault seems to be proposing a critical analysis without reformist or revolutionary possibilities for change.

Foucault's meta-history thus supposes an intellectual position which is different both from the technocratic or pragmatic use of history for institutional reform, and from a Marxist use of history for ideological criticism or for some global socialist alternative. An ideology, unlike an archaeological regularity, is assumed in Marxism to depend on the distorted assent of agents or on the functions that distorted assent serves. Thus the critique of ideology, when it demystifies the origins of our false interests, leads us to recognize our true ones, and the true ones are historically "objective"—they are the ones which somehow lead us toward *the* socialist solution, ultimately revolution. By contrast, Foucault's deep critical analysis not only does not entail any single solution or alternative, but tends to render existing proposals for change even more problematic. Foucault's meta-historical dilemma is then: how can such deep historical analysis also be a form of criticism useful in political struggles, as his intellectual commitments would seem to require.

Foucault criticizes some of the deep structures he analyzes as being *unfree,* since they rule out others. For example, he argues that our practices for grouping and interpreting art works by reference to their organistic integrity or to their authorship excludes other ways they might be read, acted upon, or "circulated." But it would seem that all deep structures are exclusionary in this way, so that the mere fact that works are received through a particular practice, even the despised humanist author-work practice, is not enough to *criticize* it. In analyzing the ways the circulation of discourse is rule-governed, Foucault would seem to have supplied no grounds for preferring one kind of circulation over another. He violently rejects the "author-function," and yet offers no alternative set of practices to take its place. Even here his rejection is not made in the name of any alternative.

The historical dilemma
While Foucault was intellectually committed to left opposition, there seems no simple way his actual historical analyses match the major schemes that have dominated *historical* thinking on the Left. Thus there has been discussion about whether and how Foucault's histories might fit within the story of the transition from feudalism to capitalism, and then to late capitalism, or the story of modernization and the rise of the bureaucracy, or the story of the growing state domination of society. Sometimes Foucault himself has speculated on how his analyses might conform to these schemes, though his periodization is evidently suited to *his* problems.

The most salient feature of this discussion of Foucault's history has been wide disagreement. For example, in American discussions, Richard Rorty, the neo-Deweyan philosopher, can castigate Foucault for a blanket resentment of the bourgeois class, while David Rothman, the social historian, can complain that he has failed to *mention* the bourgeois class in his analysis. Similarly, in France, Foucault was accused both of neglecting the state, and of making its reach so total as to leave no room for "society." One may infer that Foucault's history does not easily conform to our great stories about capitalism, bureaucracy, and the state.[2]

Moreover, Foucault's intimations of the future do not easily conform to traditional visions of the "classless society." Deep analysis, which disclaims all teleology, and which is committed to no alternatives, would not seem to provide much warrant for prophecy, prediction, or hope. And, in fact, Foucault's talk of the future usually has the form of a de-familiarizing rhetorical exercise or thought experiment. We are asked to imagine a future generation looking back with horror and disbelief at some familiar part of our activities. In a new age no one will understand any longer why on earth the mad were ever locked up and studies for several centuries, or how such peculiar entities as "Man," his "rationality," or his moral nature could have ever become central to a cultural tradition. Thus, the *History of Sexuality* ends by asking us to consider that "one day, perhaps in a different economy of bodies and pleasures"[3] people will no longer understand why for millennia we have developed a culture of the confession to sex. Little else is said about this "different economy" or about the historical or social conditions required for it to exist or to be brought about. Often, therefore, as would be consistent with "deep analysis," Foucault's talk of the future is "heterotopian" rather than "utopian," to employ a distinction from *The Order of Things*.[4] Foucault doesn't ask us to hope for a complete better form of life, but to imagine a time so different as to make our own time seem arbitrary.

But, even if we do credit Foucault with a utopian imagination, it would not be a *socialist* one. He seems to think at times that a new age is heralded by modernist art and literature in which form itself becomes central, and which may be celebrating something obscure that our enlightened time has silenced (see preceding chapter). Psychoanalysis helps us to understand what this may be, as do certain Nietzschean philosophical perspectives: our science no longer seems to embody a single and universal rationality to rid us of superstition, and the subject is but a philosophical fiction we can now do without. Thus, in the new age, science will be understood in another way, and talk of subjectivity will become as strange as it is now familiar. Foucault thus seems to envisage some post-Kantian culture which celebrates rather than confines its "madness." This vision has little in common (and, as Foucault himself suggests in his analysis of "transgression" may be *incompatible*) with such utopian ideas as the new society of the completely just distribution of goods and of work, of the unalienated satisfaction of basic human needs, of the end of the state and of all hierarchical power relations, or of idyllic rational democratic self-management.

In short, there seems no satisfactory way to insert Foucault's history within traditional left schemes, and no way to make his intimations of the future conform to socialist hopes. In addition, his method of deep historical analysis places him in an intellectual position without reform or revolution to recommend. And yet intellectually he was committed to seeing his work as a contribution to left political struggles! This is what I call Foucault's dilemma.

He became increasingly skeptical about the great models in left history, taking issue with total history and with the pretension of representing the interests of all of society. He began to argue that what now needs to be given attention in history are not the origins and functions of the state, the bureaucracy, and the corporations, but a militarization of politics and a "governmentalization" of the state. On the deep level, we need to understand modern politics as a specific and diffuse form of warfare.

I suggest that Foucault thus resolved his dilemma in adopting a "post-revolutionary" stance. I conjecture that revolution may be the vocabulary that has given us both the models by which we politically evaluate "deep" changes, and the models through which we understand the function of an intellectual in relation to the voice of a people, or to the consciousness of a class or a society.[5] By contrast, Foucault studied "deep changes" that introduce new kinds of political warfare and domination, not new institutions of peace and freedom, and he disclaimed any attempt to articulate the consciousness or voice of a people, a class, or a society. "Historical nominalism"[6] is the name I give to the methodological position consistent with this post-revolutionary outlook, and I suggest that Foucault may be the philosopher of freedom in a post-revolutionary time.

A Nominalist History

And yet freedom is precisely what many Anglo-American commentators have complained is *missing* in Foucault's history. *Discipline and Punish* confronts Clifford

Geertz with "a kind of Whig history in reverse—a history, in spite of itself, of the rise of Unfreedom."[7] Edward Thompson castigates Foucault for his "history as subject-less structure . . . in which men and women are obliterated by ideologies,"[8] a history that leads to fatalistic resignation. Foucault, historian of our unfree relation to Unfreedom.

Perhaps one reason for such misreadings is that the *kind* of freedom Foucault was interested in is unlike anything either of these two distinguished authors are looking for—not a freedom of protected *rights,* or of the good *will* gentlemen show when they agree to combat evil. Foucault formed an idea of freedom for a different intellectual and historical outlook.[9]

Foucault is assumed to propound a nominalist or anti-realist understanding of the discipline of history. He was suspicious of conceptions of historical reality which come both from traditional narrative and from the Idealist postulation of Essences which are then realized in history. He maintained that no single objective order underlies all that happens, and that there is no single aim toward which everything must tend. Which kinds of events, periods, sources, accepted inferences, styles, or problems are recognized in history are determined by the order that is imposed on the entangled mass of "documentation" with which a society is always already bound up, and it is vain to seek some further basis for them in an independent reality.

Yet nominalism was more than a methodological or philosophical preference for Foucault. His histories are *themselves* nominalist histories. They are not histories of things, but of the terms, categories, and techniques through which certain things become at certain times the focus of a whole configuration of discussion and procedure. One might say he offers a *historical* answer to the philosophical question as to how such things are "constituted." His answer is in terms not of transcendental conditions of experience, communication, or language, but of the emergence, at specific times, of assumptions common to a scattered body of thought and policy, and his aim is not to "ground" the experience of things but to denaturalize, defamiliarize, and distance us from it, and hence to question its *raison d'être.*

Thus Foucault does not write a history of madness, sickness, crime, or sex, but a history of how it ever came to be taken for granted, in a whole range of contexts, that abnormalities are kinds of mental disease, that sickness is only the dysfunction of an individual anatomy, that there exists criminal personality types it is best to lock up, or that there is something called Sex residing inside each of us as a dangerous truth that must be exposed. He writes histories of "pseudo-objects"; he uses history to dispel the sort of routine, instituted self-assurance people have about the reality of such entities as the mental disorders they fear they may be suffering from, or the inner sexual needs they believe they have to release. In questioning this reality, Foucault's histories *are* nominalist.

One of the more general targets of this de-realizing history is the group of techniques, terms, and categories that concern the subject, and, in this, Foucault's history may be seen to continue, and perhaps to radicalize, Heidegger's challenge to the post-Cartesian philosophy of the subject as well as Wittgenstein's anti-psychologism. Thus our own selves may be the great realist illusions of our time—the whole, private, individual, mental, inner entities we often take for granted as being what we are. Foucault has examined various kinds of systems of thought through which people have come to identify themselves as subjects. In the *Order of Things,* there is a long discussion of conceptions of the subject which come from our study of language, life, and work. In *Discipline and Punish,* Foucault examines the kinds of techniques through which our *bodies* have been disciplined so as to make it seem natural that an individual inner soul be ascribed to them—techniques which have thereby "fabricated" the soul as a "prison of the body."

Foucault's nominalist history, as distinct from his nominalist views *about* history, however, is not what *he* advances in his most sustained discussion of the discipline—the opening section of the *Archaeology of Knowledge.* On the contrary, he then pleaded that his work be regarded as part of an "autochthonous transformation that is taking place in the field of historical knowledge."[10] The reference is to two major developments in French history going back to the early part of the

century, each in its own way linked to Marxism, and both having been brought together by Foucault's teacher, Louis Althusser: (1) a rich tradition in the history of sciences, in which
Bachelard and Canguilhem are influential figures. This tradition, which influenced Foucault, sought to challenge the universal, objective, and progressive image of unified science
inherited from the Enlightenment through the attempt to discover an irreducible plurality of "territories" and "objects" of
knowledge, characterized by anonymous tacit procedures, and
succeeding one another through breaks and ensuing rup-
tures—a discontinuous history. (2) The "new history" identified with the journal *Annales,* which tried to put "battle-treaty"
narrative to rest, supplanting it with a broad social history
which reconstituted centuries-long continuities, eventually in a
rather quantitative manner, thus opening up new areas and new
kinds of sources (Foucault says new sorts of *events*).

It is, of course, Foucault who decides to make a
single and "autochthonous" transformation out of these two
major developments in history. He acknowledges one difference: that while ever more sharp discontinuities were being
turned up in the history of sciences, ever longer and more
"immobile" continuities in climate, price cycle, or demographic trend were being recorded within the "new history."
Surely another difference (not mentioned by Foucault) is in
attitudes toward the relative autonomy of discourses, since,
while the new historians tended to subsume discourses under
"mentalities" understood within a global picture of society, the
historians of science dealt with rather autonomous or internal-
ist traditions of scientific discourse. In fact, the connection
Foucault finds between the two kinds of history is not in a
shared understanding either of society or of knowledge.

Instead what the two share is a two-fold departure
from both the nineteenth-century historical outlook promoted
by Ranke and coinciding with the entrance of history into the
university, and the older tradition of universalist or philosophical history (whether nationalist or eventually socialist in in-
spiration). First, there is a common recognition of the
anonymity of historical events or of the fact that they can be

understood in other ways than through the traditional Aristotelian focus on human actions. Second, priority is given to
problem-solving over story-telling and an attempt is made to
separate historical continuity from the (also Aristotelian) narrative unities. The result is a new vision of the discipline itself:

> history is the work expended on material documentation (books,
> texts, accounts, registers, acts, buildings, institutions, laws, tech-
> niques, objects, customs, etc.) that exists in every time and place in
> every society either in a spontaneous or in a consciously organized
> form . . . history in its traditional form undertook to "memorize"
> the *monuments* of the past, to transform them into documents . . .
> in our time, history is that which transforms *documents* into
> *monuments* . . . .[11]

In siding with the new historians, and attempting
to transform documents into monuments, is Foucault in fact
claiming they are nominalists? His traditional historians are
realists—at least about tradition, for the events they study are
already referred to in the sources they use. By contrast, for the
new historians, a tradition is a problem, something that must
be reconstituted from a "material documentation" which is not
arranged or kept in accordance with it, and which does not
mention it as such. New historians deal with "forgotten" traditions never noticed as such. But that does not mean they are
nominalists even about the traditions they reconstitute. On the
contrary, Braudel, for example, held that his system of interlocking *durées* was the fundamental historical *reality*, in terms of
which all else, including the superficial episodes studied by
traditional historians, could be understood. He meant his history to preclude others. In claiming that Foucault writes nominalist history, I am attributing to him the view that there is *no*
single historical reality like the one Braudel envisaged, and that
his work is in this respect quite different from the *Annales*
program.

Foucault is often grouped with the new historians
as "structuralists"—historians who attempt to identify unconscious structures rather than human dramas. Foucault rejects
the linguistic analogy, arguing that there is little formal re-
semblance between a demographic trend or a scientific prob-

lematic and the formal characteristics of a language. But Foucault's history is not "structuralist" in a much stronger sense—its aim in reconstituting deep traditions is to question their very reason for existence. In this respect, Foucault would seem to depart from much of the new history, and, were he to rewrite his historiographical views, he might well attempt to *distinguish* his work from others in recent social and intellectual history through what I will describe as his conjoined use of four nominalist arguments, or four great anti-realist tropes: argument by dispersal, argument by reversal, argument by critical exposure of current practice, and argument to singular enlightenment.

1. *Dispersal.* The *Archaeology* presents nontraditional historians as rejecting a universal oneness in history that might support millennial or salvationist hopes. But Foucault's history tries to "disperse" what is presumed to be essentially whole. We have no whole lives, since there is no one thing to which all things attributed to us refers. What we call Reason and Nature are empty abstractions, since there is no one thing that all our sciences are about, and no one style of reasoning they all employ. There is no single way to classify us, our knowledge, or our world.

Consequently, history doesn't exist either: there is no one thing all our histories are about, even though there may seem nothing about which we cannot write a history. The discipline of history passes from a universal of unity or totality to a universal of disunity or plurality. Because we now think anything might have a history, it becomes implausible to think there might be one history for everything. Particular objects require particular periodizations, yet there are no periods into which all objects must fall. This is a sufficient reason to think there is no providential order underlying all that happens, and that there is nothing, not even the social being of man, that is being realized in history. In short, history is everywhere, but diffused or "in dispersion."

Accordingly, not so unlike Karl Popper, Foucault finds social holism intellectually empty (there is no such thing in history as "society as a whole") and politically dangerous (specific struggle has been "neutralized" in the hope of global transformation). He invents a politics of diffused or dispersed struggles. *Discipline and Punish* may be read as a critical analysis of at least one source of the very idea of a social whole. The theme of the book is not (as is sometimes assumed) that we all live in a totally administered society—one big Panopticon. A utopian image of a totally administered rational society can be found easily enough in Bentham, and in the more or less explicitly utilitarian reform projects Foucault analyzes. But the point of analyzing its occurrence there is precisely to dispel the realist or objective illusion that our societies *are* administered wholes. Conversely, Foucault propounds no global analysis of society of his own. His book is thus a "dispersed" analysis of one kind of preoccupation with society as a whole.

Nevertheless some assumptions even non-universalist or non-holistic historians make are challenged by Foucault, and, at one point, he says that what he really wants is "to do the history of the 'objectivication' of those elements historians take as objectively given."[12] This is a prescription for *reversal*.

2. *Reversal*. An instance of reversal is found in Foucault's very first work about madness when he rebukes historians for using psychiatric categories to understand, for example, witchcraft or magic, in pre-psychiatric societies. A reversal of this approach provides him with the main question of his own work: in what ways has the constitution of the object "mental illness" supposed and established forms of domination in our own society? The first volume of his history of sexuality offers another instance of reversal. It starts with the nominalist thesis that there is no such thing as sex in itself, and then proceeds by a reversal of history that rests on the "repressive hypothesis." A whole style of history takes for granted that sex and its repression are self-evident, and then looks back into the past to discover how the second befell the first. Foucault reverses this approach and asks how did sex ever become "objectivized" as an object of knowledge and practice in the first place, and how did we ever arrive at the paradoxical task of working hard to "liberate" something that our history had in fact misled us into thinking was real.

The most far-reaching case of Foucault's reversal, however, is in *political* history. He proposes to reverse a centuries-long tradition in political thought which he calls "sovereignty-theory." Thus, he formulates an analysis of power that is "the exact opposite of Hobbes."[13] Instead of proposing a new science of politics, he tries to understand how a political science itself could emerge and assume its hold over our current practices. Instead of asking how a multiplicity of subjects come together to form a constitution to determine that sovereignty which unites them, he asks how we have been "really and materially" constituted as subjects: in the case of disciplines, as *individuals,* and in the case of bio-power, as a *population* with the recorded and measured variables modern governments must now know about their own territories as well as those of their rivals. He also examines how life and welfare (or happiness) became constituted as political entities a government must directly pursue and administer, rather than something undetermined which should result from good statesmanship. He claims that "police science" was one of the first kinds of knowledge of the populations of modern states, and that in it may lie the origins of the Marxist categories of the forces and relations of production. He analyzes the categories of police science in conjunction with a post-Machiavellian discussion of the reason or rationality of states in order to show that excessive attention has been given to "the genesis of the State, its history, its power and abuses, etc."[14] The state has been seen as a *monstre froid* or as the apparatus to reproduce exploitative relations of production, with the consequence that a central political task was to take it over and abolish it. Foucault thinks we need to reverse this tendency and ask how the state ever came to be constituted as our main enemy:

> But the State, probably no more today than at any other time in its history, does not have this unity, this individuality, this rigorous functionality, nor, to speak frankly, this importance; maybe after all the State is no more than a composite reality and a mystical abstraction whose importance is a lot more limited than many of us think. Maybe what is really important for our modern times, that is, for our actuality, is not so much the State domination of society, but the "governmentalization" of the State.[15]

Many kinds of political history take the existence of the individual, the state, the people, the population, as self-evident, whole, real entities. Foucault tries to reverse this self-evidence, asking how such entities have been "really and materially" constituted or objectivized, in much the same way as he tries to reverse the assumptions of the repressive hypothesis by asking how sex itself has been constituted or objectified. In both instances, the reversal is meant to be a politically consequential one, and, more generally, Foucault's nominalism is intended as a form of criticism.

3. *Critique.* Normally, critique is historical when its standards are placed either in the past or in the future. But such nostalgic or prophetic critique rests on a form of history that predicts or explains as Foucault's does not. In his nominalist history, writing about the past *is* a way of criticizing the present under the assumption that the past still informs the present in ways and with consequences we don't recognize. Thus, though it scarcely advances beyond the nineteenth century, *Discipline and Punish* calls itself a "history of the present." The formula assumes a wider application. The "present" refers to those things that are constituted in our current proceedings in ways we don't realize are rooted in the past, and writing a "history" of it is to lay bare that constitution and its consequences. The point of Foucault's history of our categories of the criminal personality or of our practices of incarceration is thus neither to explain the past nor to learn moral lessons from it. Foucault does not show our situation to be a lawlike outcome of previous ones, or to have been necessitated by the latest historical "conjuncture." On the contrary, he tries to make our situation seem less "necessitated" by history, and more peculiar, unique, or arbitrary.

Foucault's nominalist history might thus be said to be critical in that it studies the past in order to find alternatives to the present. Yet it is not about the alternatives themselves. It neither looks for them in the past nor projects them into the future. In de-realizing objects, or showing with what consequences we assume them to be real, Foucault would try to open up a discussion of alternatives which his history would not itself predetermine. He uses history to make the "realities" of our current practices seem arbitrary or contingent; that is his critique. His is therefore a "singularizing" history, not a universal one.

4. *Singular enlightenment.* Foucault saw himself as perpetuating the principle whereby philosophers "enlighten" their present, which Kant introduced in his classic 1784 paper that defines Enlightenment as an emancipation from self-imposed "immaturity."[16] But while Foucault may have tried to enlighten our present, he was hardly a figure of *the* Enlightenment. Indeed he is often taken as the great modern counter-Enlightenment philosopher and historian.

More precisely Foucault's nominalism is directed against the *universalism* of the Enlightenment. He rejects identification of enlightenment with a unified science whose universal conditions would reside in Man. He tries to disperse the purported Unity of all sciences, and to reverse the assumptions of philosophical anthropology by asking how such enormous importance could have been attributed to the rather strange entity we call Man. By contrast, he finds the conditions of our knowledge, in particular, contingent and anonymous regularities. In thus criticizing the conditions of scientific discourse about such entities as "mental illness" or "the criminal personality," he is not rejecting science as such or criticizing *all* rational discourse. Foucault also tries to reverse assumptions in histories that tell of the moral progress of introducing universalist humanitarian principles into the treatment or correction of criminals and madmen. He asks how the reform projects in fact contributed to the constitution of something that might be called universal humanity. Similarly he asks how the projects contributed to our idea of a whole and universal society—something he himself "disperses" into a range of different practices. Thus, he criticizes "enlightened" correctional practices, but does not reject *all* talk of human dignity or decency. In reversing, dispersing, and criticizing what was taken to be universal, Foucault attacks what, in the present, has come to be regarded as *the* Enlightenment.

Thus Foucault is suspicious of the universalist vocation of the intellectual. In his paper on Enlightenment, Kant envisages a republican government for which a universal enlightened public would become a kind of conscience. There would be the public, published exchange among those writers (*grammaticos*) who had emancipated themselves from any authority except universal reason itself. It is not just that Foucault does not share Kant's vision of history as the progressive enlightenment and emancipation of Man. It is not just that he finds that our actual "governmentalities" are quite distant from classical republicanism. Foucault doesn't find emancipation in a universalist maturity, the ability to escape all unreason. Rather, for Foucault, freedom lies in our capacity to find alternatives to the particular forms of discourse that define us by reference, among other things, to universal humanity. Instead of finding enlightenment in universal Reason or Society, he finds it in uncovering the particularity and contingency of our knowledge and our practices.

Edward Thompson tries to defend some kind of voluntarism against what he takes to be Foucault's structuralism. "Men and women" must somehow be held responsible for determining their own history, or be completely resigned to it. I have presented Foucault not as a structuralist but as a historical nominalist, and have maintained that what he denies is not that there is freedom in history, but that organized and deliberate struggles of some "collective will" articulated by intellectuals are the only source of it. In fact, the assumption that we will be free only when we completely *control* our history may belong to a specific kind of intellectual discourse—one in which it is assumed that there exists something whole and universal called the masses, the people, or society, whose interests the intellectual represents or demystifies, whose voice or consciousness he articulates, whose better life he envisages in utopias, and by reference to whose sovereignty he makes judgments and looks with confidence into the future. The despair attributed to Foucault's history may be only the other side of this confidence—despair over the unfree society only the result of a confidence in the cause of a completely free and rational one. Both may be products of the kind of "revolutionary discourse" to which Foucault's nominalist history is in fact opposed.

Post-Revolutionary Politics

There is an obvious contrast between Foucault's nominalist history and discourses about revolution. In a revolutionary discourse, critical analysis always leads to the necessity for one and the same radical or global transformation, whereas nominalist history is critical analysis committed to no transformational scheme at all. The contrast may be pursued philosophically, intellectually, and historically.

Philosophically, the nominalist sees freedom in a deep anonymous *contingency* in his present, whereas the revolutionary sees it in the promise or the necessity of a new regime—he is confident that history must move toward a freer state, which usually means one that is more self-conscious, self-controlled, or self-managed. The nominalist does not see freedom as something history must *realize* but something that threatens to *dissolve* what history has presented as necessary or progressive. And thus he believes that history has no *end*. Many sacrifices have been made for the free society at the end of history and the nominalist can be rather skeptical about them.

Intellectually, the nominalist may attempt to show the contingency of deep historical configurations in his time in order to make it more difficult for them to survive. But he does not thereby *represent* any group that figures within the configuration, for in fact the assumption of his analysis is that no such group can be the agent of the change of the configuration. Unlike the revolutionary intellectual he does not see his work as representing a group or a class or even a society in which there would be no more classes.

The nominalist and revolutionary outlooks thus rest on contrasting conceptions of *history*. For the nomalist recognizes no necessary movement or total periodizations in history, and is concerned with a kind of change which is anonymous and nondeliberate.

Thus, in the first place, there is nothing like the class struggle or the social emancipation of mankind to be the "motor" of history. The diffuse configurations of power do not play the role of driving world history onwards, unlike the

Marxist idea of contradiction between relations and forces of production. On the contrary, it is only within one such config-uration tht the categories of relations and forces of production occur. Even the history of informal knowledge is not a history of Kuhnian *revolutions*. As Ian Hacking points out, "for all his talk of 'irruptions' and so forth" Foucault does not explain change in terms of the accumulation of anomalies internal to a tradition.[17] His history is not about the "essential tension" between innovation and tradition. For Foucault, nothing grows or evolves internally; and nothing stays or endures. Fur-thermore the nominalist is anti-universalist, and so maintains that there is no universal history to realizes a completely free society which a people may be destined to carry out. There is no universal history, there is no completely free society, and there is no destiny of a people.

For, in the second place, the premise of the nomi-nalist analysis of "power" is that historically there is no essen-tial, natural, or inevitable way of grouping or classifying people, nothing that a state of nature might be used to de-scribe. We are not born free; we are always already thrown into some configuration of power. Hence what one should study in history are the anonymous deep configurations that determine the ways we are classified and grouped—the deep history of the constitution of our "polities." On the deep level what con-stitutes our polities is an anonymous strategic configuration, the surface of which is irreducibly dispersed. On that level, no group or class is sovereign; no group or class is the agent of change. Thus freedom does not basically lie in discovering or being able to determine who we are, but in rebelling against those ways in which we are already defined, categorized, and classified.

Therefore, a nominalist historian can have no global scheme of transformation to propose, and no people or no society as a whole whose interests he can represent. He is in no position to talk about revolution.

Traditionally in revolutionary discourse there is a scheme for the political analysis of global historical change in which sovereignty is assigned to some group or class whose interests (voice, consciousness) intellectuals represent, articulate, legitimate, and so forth. In the famous events in France, when the word "revolution" first acquired its secular and political meaning and when utopia acquired more than a literary importance, we find the discourse that postulates a new beginning (or "clearing") in which *everything* is politicized or is seen as part of the same great world-historical transformation symbolized in a new sovereignty—in this case the people whose existence in the state of nature had been so much debated. A history in the nominalist style might be written about how this discourse was taken up, transformed, betrayed in its movement through the Commune to Russia and even to China and Cuba. Principles for such a history are to be found in Foucault.

In the first place, the revolutionary self-interpretation of the period in France from the Bastille to Napoleon is not what Foucault's deep analysis of power records. It is true that the *Birth of the Clinic* analyzes an "event" in the history of medicine that occurs in just this period, and that introduces a change more radical than anything since Greek medicine—a whole new conception of disease, new ways to study it, new social relations between doctor and patient, the replacement of a "holistic" tradition with one centered on the examination of the anatomy of each individual. The point, however, is that the clinic which was born in this way was not required either by history or by reason, and we may have yet other kinds of medicine. Moreover, in Foucault's subsequent work, one discovers to what degree medicine becomes one of the main foci for changes in configurations of power. The control of epidemics and the reorganization of the hospital contribute to the implantation of discipline, while public health policies become one of the great sources of bio-power—eventually medicine was to play an important part in modern racisms.

Thus, in *Discipline and Punish,* about which historians have complained that "the revolutionary period is strangely erased,"[18] Foucault explicitly advances the counter-Enlightenment theme which so impressed Geertz: "The eighteenth century doubtless invented our liberties; but it gave them a profound and solid underpinning—the disciplinary society from which we still derive."[19] The "rights" which were legally instituted during the Revolution in fact became part of a disciplinary power configuration—the new, more efficient, downward-looking, normalizing, and individualizing "network" of practice Foucault calls "discipline." If this network resembles Weber's famous "iron-cage," its analysis stresses that it is autonomous, anonymous, programmatic, and dispersed. It is assumed that "punitive methods" are autonomous and are "not simply . . . consequences of legislation or indicators of social structure." Rather they are "techniques possessing their own specificity within the more general field of other ways of excercising power," and as such cannot be explained by reference to a class or its ideal type.[20] A diffuse yet autonomous "network" gradually subordinates or colonizes the legal institutions and the sociological knowledge of crime for the purpose of imposing order rather than for forbidding or protecting.

In short, assuming that there is a "period" of revolution, its role in Foucault's deep history of power is either to reinforce or to mask the implantation of discipline and of biopower.

One way the inheritance from the period masks or obscures the power configurations of our era, in the second place, is philosophical or intellectual. When Foucault claims "we have not yet cut off the King's head in political theory," he means that we still tend to take some version of the idea of the people (e.g., our real social nature) as constitutive of who or what is (or should be) sovereign, and that this in fact has prevented us from identifying, on a deep level, what is decisive for the politics of our present. Hence there is a gap between our political thinking (and our role as political intellectuals) and a basic historical and political reality in our times. In particular there is a gap between the revolutionary discourse, in which a concept of sovereignty is still central, and the deep analysis of anonymous forms of power. Thus we need to turn to Nietzsche for a "philosophy of power that does not enclose it within a political theory."[21]

The philosophical gap is closed in several ways in Foucault. First, in effect, he maintains that there can be no nonutopian society that is totally free. The very idea of a totally free society is utopian, and utopia is to be understood nominalistically as a discursive effect or as the affirmation of an intellectualist misconception of history. In his debate with Foucault, Chomsky argues that a utopia is inscribed in the deep universal structures of language. Foucault retorts that the "deep structures" he studies in *discourse* are specific and implicated in power, and *they* are what we need to study in history.

Second, "rights" are to be interpreted nominalistically in terms of the configuration of power in which they figure, rather than realistically in terms of the real nature of our humanity or our society. Thus, while "civil rights" have become embedded within disciplinary power, "social rights" have become involved in bio-political struggles. Foucault argues that the utopian language which refers to the real social "ontology" of needs and labor is "of little importance" in understanding those rights and their contribution to rebellion against the "political administration of life."[22] The relevant notions of needs and works are in fact determined by that administration. Historically, social rights are different from those civil ones that can be protected by enforcing the correlative duties, not because they point toward the society revolution will provide us, but because of the struggles they introduce in the configuration of power that has made the nature of Man and of his life into key political targets. More generally, freedoms must be understood in more basic terms than the guarantee for civil or social rights—in terms of the actual struggles in which they figure: "All the forms of liberty, acquired or claimed, all the rights which one values, even those involving the least important of matters, doubtlessly find in revolt a last point on which to anchor themselves, one that is more solid and near than natural rights."[23] Revolt and not revolution.

In the third place, the configurations of power Foucault has studied predate, survive, and help to determine the nature of the Yalta geopolitical divide. Neither "socialism" nor "capitalism" has been able to do without them; the international politics of armaments are part of them. They are compatible both with democratic and nondemocratic political forms, though different political regimes have adapted them in different ways, in East and West Europe, in Latin and North America.

Therefore, the configurations of power may be what characterize modern politics and make a particular political regime into a modern one. Perhaps ours is not the era of a great competition among rival political ideologies. On the contrary, it may be the era in which there is a general devaluation and delegitimization of all political ideologies at the hands of the political *technologies* on which they increasingly rely—technologies that are autonomous on a deep level while dispersed on the surface. Perhaps it is these technologies which have spelled an end to discourses of revolution, and that is why we need to devise the instruments to analyze them historically.

In any case, far from determining what is or should be sovereign in our society, Foucault has introduced a conception of power as a deep strategic configuration in which classes or groups are never controlling agents, the change of which is "not acquired once and for all by a new control of the apparatuses nor by a new functioning or a destruction of the institutions; on the other hand, none of its localized episodes may be inscribed in history except by the effects that it induces on the entire network in which it is caught up."[24]

No single episode, no single network is historically necessary or irreversible, and in all episodes and networks there is always revolt and rebellion, both actual and potential. If in no particular instance is power ever necessary or assured, it never changes all at once or is eliminated once and for all. Therefore a fight is going on at all times in everything—bodies, customs, laws, languages, morals, arts, and so on. Nominalist history is the history of such fights, their deep strategies, the *wars* that interconnect them. It is not a history of tradition or of progress, for at bottom it knows only the "hazards of the battle." Foucault proposes to invert Clausewitz's formula and to regard politics as warfare continued through other means: "war [doesn't] exhaust itself in its own contradictions and end by renouncing violence and submitting to civil laws. On the contrary . . . humanity installs each of its violences in a system of rules, and thus proceeds from domination to domination."[25] We need history to analyze our modern political warfare, not to remind us of revolutionary promises. For there is no war that will put an end to all domination. There is no Revolution.

Freeing Pierre

Foucault speaks of an irony in the history of sex— namely the fact that we have been led to believe that our liberation was, in any way, at issue. Matching this irony *in* his history is the irony *of* his history—that his deep historical analysis, which has intellectual roots in Marx and which was acclaimed in a left political culture, should end up with a critical analysis of the very discourse of liberation and revolution.

In 1973 Foucault republished a case from the rather gruesome pages of the *Annales d'hygiène publique et de médecine légale* of 1836. There are some fragments of a *Mémoire* by a barely literate peasant boy in which he premeditates and recounts his murder of his mother, sister, and brother in an obscure French village. Entitled *I, Pierre Rivière,* the *Mémoire* is published together with a conflictual discussion among various authorities who find witnesses in their debate over whether the boy is criminal or insane, and with some commentary and evaluation by Foucault and a team of French social historians. Retrospectively, the whole work may be read as a peculiar and involved allegory of Foucault's historical project.

In Foucault's writings the work occurs between his great contribution to intellectual history, *Les Mots et les choses* of 1966, and his great contribution to social history, *Surveiller et punir* of 1975. In each case the contribution was part of an ongoing historiographic reflection which leads to what I call the nominalist analysis of power. Thus the work appeared as Foucault was formulating the principles that would lead him to detect the irony of our discourse about sexual liberation.

While it is representative of a general left insistence that history study the downtrodden rather than the elite, *I, Pierre Rivière* also illustrates Foucault's own preoccupations.

The work is as much historiographic as it is historical. It includes the very sources it discusses. The sources are used not to establish the facts of the case, but to determine what precisely made it into a *case*. They support a general hypothesis not about the nature of crime in French society, but about the discourses dealing with crime and, more precisely, about the deep configuration by which an entity like "criminal insanity" was constituted. In short, the sources are used for a nominalist history. The power or politics to which Foucault refers is not the power of the experts but of their *discourses*.

The nominalist approach is what enables Foucault's perversity in treating the *Mémoire* neither as a piece of sociological evidence nor as a case of political injustice, but as a kind of found poem to be read for its rare "beauty," which induces "utter astonishment" and for its "peculiar power of derangement." Part of this astonishing beauty and deranging power lies precisely in Pierre's *act* of writing. Foucault points out that without the killings and their punishment Rivière's jottings would not have constituted the same act of writing, and could not have become a case. The strange beauty partially derives from the strange tradition in which the act of writing occurs— namely the criminological debate. Fiercely anti-hermeneutic principles must be adopted to properly "read" the case: "Since the principle governing their existence and coherence is neither that of a composite work nor a legal text, the outdated academic methods of textual analysis and all the concepts which are the appanage of the dreary and scholastic prestige of writing on writing can very well be eschewed in studying them."[26]

Hence the irony: that the work of a completely forgotten, almost illiterate young crazed killer should turn out to be a wonderous work that ended up securing for its author the glory that history had seemed to have denied him. Following Foucault's republication of his work, Pierre Rivière became the hero of a film acclaimed in a left political culture.

Though he may have anticipated neither, Pierre Rivière has become both a *case* and an *author*. Foucault stresses that his actual crime was not extraordinary (but rather common), and that he was neither an important nor a popular person. In fact, his very insignificance and lack of popularity is important for Foucault's argument, since it helps to put in a naked and ridiculing light the mad administrative machinery used to investigate his case. In this sense, Pierre resembles what Foucault later calls "les hommes infâmes," actual rogues about whom nothing more is known than what was recorded in various police and administrative sources. Unlike the *fama* or popular criminal heroes, the life of such men is perfectly suited for a nominalist history, since it is literally "constituted" through sources such as the *lettre de cachet* designed to weed it out. Hence it is ironic that Pierre should posthumously acquire the *fama* of an author.

There are then two ways of reading the purport of the case: (1) it is incredible that our culture is so obsessed with criminal insanity that it was tracking it down more than a century ago in the miserable life of a completely insignificant peasant boy; (2) it is strange that only through a criminological interrogation this rare and beautiful work has come down to us. On the first reading Foucault's point would be that it is disturbing that our culture finds works like Pierre's to be strangely beautiful, and that is what requires analysis. On the second reading the point would be that the work *is* strangely beautiful and belongs to a counter-tradition including such heroes as Artaud and Sade which our outmoded literary culture has suppressed. In short the problem is: to what political culture does Pierre belong as an *author* given that it is clear to what culture he belongs as a *case*?

In fact, the case of Pierre Rivière is an excellent illustration of Foucault's nominalist analysis of power. Foucault insists that we regard the *Mémoire* as an "event that provided the intersection of discourses that differed in origin, form, organization and function." It provided the battleground for a "battle among discourses and through discourses." It became part of a "history in which there are no rulers . . . below the level of power."[27] The diversity or dispersion in origin, form, organization, and function demonstrates that the emergence of the battle is free though nondeliberate. No one and nothing is responsible for the event itself, though the issue of responsibility and free will occurs inside the debate over Pierre's possible insanity.

Hence the *Mémoire* is an "event" in a non-Aristotelian sense. It is not the unfolding of a drama whose plot (*diegesis*) weaves together great speeches and acts of heroic characters into a pattern of fate. It is a singular clash among various kinds of discourse, a story without heroes, villians, or fate—a battle without a stage. The power it involves is not the power of the characters but of the discourses devised to describe them.

From *Discipline and Punish* one learns that this "battle" was part of a larger warfare, a deep strategic configuration, the surface of which was dispersed throughout many different institutions in France; its aim was to constitute the "criminal personality" on which a whole system of incarceration and a whole "field of power" in society would be based. It is thus an unheroic war waged by unsuspecting if uninspiring local technocrats dispersed in various institutions, whose projects fell into a strategic pattern than can be attributed to no one group's interests or intentions. It is a "political" configuration in that it classified people in such a way as to make them governable. Disciplines are the various techniques that constitute a "deep" strategy for sorting people into disciplined, individualized, manageable groups—as in a military parade. *Discipline and Punish* is the story of the triumph of this kind of warfare over others.

> In short, to substitute for a power that is manifested through the brilliance of those who exercise it, a power that insidiously objectifies those on whom it is applied; to form a body of knowledge about these individuals, rather than to deploy the ostentatious signs of sovereignty.[28]

Thus power in the most fundamental instance is not found in forms of government or ruling elites, but is paradoxically a depth property of activites that are *not* political. For the power of governments *over* societies always relies on a deep power *within* society, such that "power always comes from below."

Therefore, "politics" in culture or arts does not consist in positions, attitudes, or dependencies on governments. The fundamental "political" question about a work is not what political view it embodies or articulates, what vision of society as a whole it proposes or assumes, or what "aesthetic" qualities transport it above all political controversy. Rather, it is a question of the "depth configuration" of power it supports of challenges in its topics but also in its forms and its "intertextuality." Thus Foucault considers works political where form itself is at issue, in an almost Brechtian sense that they thereby challenge conditions of reception and production. In particular, he endorses works, such as fragments, which question the principle of organistic integrity, or automatic writing, which questions the principle of authorial intention—both "deep" principles of a humanist politics.

At first, Foucault primarily identified a politics of high and avant-gardist culture. As he began to identify deep configurations of power in social history, however, the boundaries of what is "cultural" became blurred, and works like crime novels were discussed. What is political *in* a culture was no longer what was political about the culture as such. Thus one might well argue that a "politics of internalization" (like the one shown in the psychologization of crime in the Rivière case) runs through many aspects of modern cultural productions—the aesthetic principle that art is a form of internal discovery or examination, the actual techniques of self-interrogation it employs or introduces, the sense it gives that our inner secrets have to be desires about sexual deviance, crime, insanity, violence, and the like. Works, which obey this principle, which have these techniques or induce this sense, would belong to the same deep configuration that constitutes the category of an "inner personality" as in the Rivière case. Thus we might speculate that the "beauty" of Rivière fragmentary formulation of his incestuous crimes is that it offers an "objective correlative" for what we are led to imagine is secretly going on inside us, and that it involves the same "deep politics" that induced the investigation of his case in the first place. In short, Pierre as author would be part of the same culture as Pierre as *case* after all.

In any event, this is the irony of Foucault's dilemma, the irony of an intellectual stance which is neither pragmatic nor revolutionary, without authority, charismatic or bureaucratic, without authorship or any guide for policy. It is a position of radical freedom. It is from this position that Foucault imagines himself to be pursued—not so unlike the infamous Pierre Rivière. Right after 1968 he declared:

Do not ask who I am and do not ask me to remain the same: leave it to our bureaucrats and our police to see that our papers are in order. At least spare us their morality when we write.[29]

Notes

1. Michel Foucault, *The Order of Things,* p. xiv.
2. "Discipline" has been identified both with the administration of the state and with institutional arrangements out of its protective reach no doubt because it problematizes traditional *political* alternatives. The relative autonomy of the "technologies" of power and their apparent compatibility with different forms of government raise a political dilemma: neither a Leninist capture of the state nor the alternative democratic (parliamentary or council) politics seems able to combat the disciplinary. Cf. Poulantzas, n. 15.

The case for the protective state is made by Michael Walzer (*Dissent,* Fall 1983), who accuses Foucault of repeating observations about the increased administrative organization of society that he (Walzer) and others made fifteen years ago; moreover, Foucault does this, he says, in an "importantly wrong" fashion since no room is left for the "political philosophy and philosophical jurisprudence" that, to Walzer and others, set limits on that organization. In short, Foucault is said to be unaware of the liberal state, with no way to distinguish ordinary prisoners in our liberal jails from students in school, workers in a factory, or, more seriously, political prisoners in totalitarian jails. Walzer fails to see, however, that a "positive evaluation of the liberal state" is no real way out of Foucault's dilemma: (1) He is unaware of what Foucault *has* said about liberalism and its relation to the "governmentalization of the State." (2) He incorrectly assumes that the argument in *Discipline and Punish* commits Foucault to "Marxist functionalism." In fact, Foucault cites several *Annales* historians about new forms of criminality for which he thinks several "technologies" were devised; the disciplinary triumphed because of the ways it "continues and intensifies" techniques in other parts of society. The point is not that the disciplinary is necessitated by capitalism, but that it is not *necessary* at all. (3) Walzer makes very questionable use of the totalitarian thesis as a kind of blackmail against new sorts of criticism of prisons in the great liberal state. Foucault would no doubt contest that thesis as an *obstacle* to understanding the specific politics of East European socialism and the resistance to it.

3. Foucault, *The History of Sexuality,* p. 159.

4. *The Order of Things,* p. xviii: *"Utopias* afford consolation: although they have no real locality, there is nevertheless a fantastic, untroubled region in which they are able to unfold: they open up cities with vast avenues, superbly planted gardens, countries where life is easy, even though the road to them is chimerical. *Heterotopias* are disturbing, probably because they secretly undermine language, because they make it impossible to name this *and* that, because they shatter or tangle common names, because they destroy syntax in advance, and not only the syntax with which we construct sentences but also the less apparent syntax which causes words and things (next to and also opposite one another) to hold together. That is why utopias permit fables and discourse: they run with the very grain of language and are part of the fundamental dimension of the *fabula;* heterotopias (such as those to be found in Borges) dessicate speech, stop words in their tracks, contest the very possibility of grammar at its source; they dissolve our myths and sterilize the lyricism of our sentences."

5. In *Le Monde* (May 11, 1979), Foucault himself contrasts revolution with revolt: "The age of revolution has arrived. That realization has hung over history for two centuries, organizing our perception of time and polarizing our hopes. It has shaped a colossal effort to become accustomed to revolt as interior to a history that is regarded as both rational and controllable. It has granted revolt a legitimacy, while sorting out its good from its bad forms. It has fixed its preliminary conditions, established its objectives and the ways in which they will be realized. Even the profession of the revolutionary has been defined. In repatriating revolt, one has claimed to have manifested its truth and to have brought it to its real issue. A marvelous and formidable promise." In calling Foucault a "postrevolutionary," I mean he attempted to problematize this promise and to defend the specificity of revolt—and of the kinds of power it confronts. I am *not* attributing to him some version of a thesis, common to Irving Kristol and Hannah Arendt, that there are two revolutions—the French, which leads to totalitarianism, and the American, which leads to liberal democracy. I think Foucault would dispute the totalitarian thesis on which this idea of two revolutions depends, and would claim that we need to devise forms of struggle appropriate to the specific "technologies" which confront us—that, for example, East European socialism as well as, say, Latin American dictatorship involve specific kinds of "political rationality" and require specific forms of ."revolt." Like the theory of revolution, the theory of totalitarianism has prevented us from seeing this specificity. Thus Foucault would hold that our real problem is one of political technologies, not political ideologies.

6. In *L'Impossible Prison,* Foucault describes himself as a historical nominalist (p. 56): "As Paul Veyne has seen, it is a question of the effects on historical knowledge of a nominalist critique that is itself formulated through a historical analysis." The reference is to "Foucault révolutionne l'histoire,"

where Veyne finds rarefaction to be the aim of Foucault's history: "to understand that things are only objectifications of determined practices, the determinations of which need to be exposed, since consciousness has no conception of them . . ." (*Comment on écrit l'histoire*, p. 219). Veyne cites Duns Scotus, somewhat paradoxically, since Scotus held that there *are* natural kinds or terms that refer to a *communis naturae* which is then "individualized" in each instance of the kind (*haeccicity*). Nominalism is usually taken to refer to the doctrine, propounded in the Middle Ages, that only individual things exist and that the way they are sorted into classes is only a convention of human practice, an assumption of human language, or an invention of the human mind. In formulating a "nominalist critique" through a *historical* analysis, Foucault would rule out the inference that "names" such as "the mad" or "the criminal personality" are just fictions of the mind or creatures of language, for the practices in which they are "determined," while not conceived by consciousness, are taken to be quite real. It is this reality of the practice in which names figure that is capable of transformation, which, however, cannot be effected through mere linguistic change or voluntarist fiat. In this senses, the "names" themselves would be "material." Thus Foucault would undo the subjective turn that might be associated with Kant when he tried to make "realism" contrast not with nominalism but with *idealism* (a distant consequence being the Marxist epic of materialism vs. idealism).

In *Vocabulaire technique et critique de la philosophie,* Henri Lande reports that already at the end of the nineteenth century a *nominalisme scientifique* held that science was not unified and that reality was whatever objective discourse refers to. This accords with Foucault's *nominalist critique* except that it is not simply a matter of "warranted assertability," since consciousness does not have a conception of what determines the reference to an object. Foucault's nominalism is in fact applied primarily to cases in which we ourselves are sorted into classes. Here Duns Scotus *is* a precursor, since he held that as individuals we are free not because of a common nature (our bodies are free in this sense). Foucault, however, historicizes the issue of how we acquire a "nature," and does not have recourse to the love of God to reconstitute a unity. Finally, Veyne does not see that such nominalism leads to what I call Foucault's dilemma. Foucault, he says, also "de-revolutionizes" history since "the disappearance of the objectification 'the mad' does not depend on our will, even our revolutionary will, but . . . obviously presupposes a metamorphosis of practices on a scale for which the word 'revolution' would only denote a pale zeal" (p. 227). But since revolution is precisely total, the reference to scale seems curious. The myth of a metamorphosis greater and more intense even than a revolution has, of course, lent its cover to the abstract and symbolic forms of the "postpolitical" or "micropolitical" gesturing which sometimes invokes Foucault.

7. Clifford Geertz, in *The New York Review of Books,* Jan. 26, 1978.

8. E. P. Thompson, *The Poverty of Theory* (New York: Monthly Review Press, 1978).

9. In the last chapter, I reconstruct a conception of freedom implicit in Foucault, according to two principles: (1) de-anthropologization, or the

thesis that we are free not in having a nature (place in tradition, etc.) but in being able to reject and transform what is presented to us *as* our nature; and (2) the antinomy between real and nominal freedoms, or the thesis that any formal or instituted liberty is part of a larger complex of practices that engages our "real" freedom only to reject and transform it. If utopian thought attempts to provide the ideal case where formal and real freedoms coincide, "nominalist" history tries to increase our real freedom by demonstrating the specific ways in which our nominal freedoms *are* in fact nominal.

10. Foucault, *The Archaeology of Knowledge*, p. 15.

11. *Ibid.*, p. 71.

12. *L'Impossible Prison*, p. 55.

13. Foucault, *Power/Knowledge*, p. 102.

14. "On Governmentality," *I&C*, no. 6, p. 20.

15. *Ibid.* In *State, Power, and Socialism* (London: NLB, 1978), Poulantzas regards the Leninist ideas of the vanguard party, of the opposition revolution or reform and of democracy as dictatorship of the bourgeoisie, as bankrupt; our real problem is statism. Foucault is a useful corrective to the traditional analysis of the state, however, since his "power relations" don't emanate from the state, but are dispersed in society and "do not exhaust class relations and may go a certain way beyone them" (Poulantzas, p. 43). To Poulantzas, Foucault makes these power relations so autonomous that there can be no *political* solution, and this in turn leads to ineffectual nihilism. To such charges, Foucault can respond that there is no general answer to the question of how power technologies come to form a part of the administration of states (though a central way is through the network for the administration of populations). Each case requires a historical and political analysis linked with local forms of resistance. Foucault may not have a clearly articulated politics of parties, bureaucracies, and so forth, but that may not only be *his* dilemma; it may be a more general dilemma for the formulation of political strategies today.

16. Foucault, "Georges Canghilhem, Philosopher of Error."

17. Ian Hacking, "Foucault's Immature Science," in *Nous* (1979), no. 13, p. 79.

18. Foucault, *L'Impossible Prison*, p. 11.

19. This statement appears on the dust cover of *Surveiller et punir.*

20. Foucault, *Discipline and Punish*, p. 23. On Weber, cf. *L'Impossible Prison*, p. 48, passim: "'Discipline' is not the expression of an 'ideal type' (that of 'disciplined man'); it is the generalization and interconnecting of different techniques that themselves respond to local objectives"

21. *Power/Knowledge*, p. 121.

22. *The History of Sexuality*, p. 145.

23. *Le Monde*, May 11, 1979.

24. *Discipline and Punish*, p. 27.

25. Foucault, *Language, Counter-Memory, Practice*, p. 151. Cf. *Power/Knowledge*, pp. 90–91: "This reversal of Clausewitz's assertion that war is politics continued by other means has a triple significance: . . . [1] it consists in seeing politics as sanctioning and upholding the disequilibrium of forces that

was displayed in war. . . . [2] none of the political struggles . . . within this "civil peace" . . . should be interpreted except as the continuation of war. . . . [3] the end result can only be the outcome of war, that is, of a contest of strength, to be decided in the last analyses by recourse to arms. . . . Only a final battle of that kind would put an end, once and for all, to the exercise of power as continual war."

26. *I, Pierre Rivière,* p. xi.
27. *Ibid.,* p. x.
28. *Discipline and Punish,* p. 220.
29. *The Archaeology of Knowledge,* p. 17.

CHAPTER THREE

The Transformation of Critique

Critical Struggles

Foucault directs his nominalist history to a particular kind of struggle that assumes a very distinctive form in the postwar period. He refers to struggles which, while their organizational forms vary according to different economies and political institutions, share a number of common features: they are concerned with direct or concrete effects of power on people's lives and bodies; they involve unrecognized or unanalyzed operations of domination; they are not subordinated to long-range social solutions typical of an older left outlook; they involve not simply disinformation and mystification but the very forms and privileges of knowledge; their central issue is subjectivity.[1]

In Germany and France at least, "theory" or philosophy played a role in such struggles in a way that the dominant analytic philosophy in English-speaking countries did not. Philosophy was used in these struggles, and the struggles were used to question the philosophical tradition. "Critique" is the usual term applied to such philosophy. If "critique" names the exposure of unrecognized operations of power in people's lives, then Foucault was certainly engaged in critique, or was a critical theorist.

But as the use of thought Foucault makes in these struggles is a singular one, so is his kind of critique. His critique is at some distance from the leftist mania of warring "positions" and "lines." For his thinking or theory has an analytic but not a justificatory role. He offers no political line, but attempts to rethink the experiences around which political struggles crystallize. He writes not so much *with* the struggles as *about* the things they problematize. His "theory" is directed to an analysis of the problematization of experience in concrete historical situations; it does not assume the form of a general or abstract criticism of state and economy.

If Foucault rarely uses the word "critique" or describes himself as a "critical theorist," it is in part because his critique is of a new and specific sort which does not employ the familiar language of alienation, mystification, and repression. The nature of the more traditional theory concerned with the critique of ideology and repression has been formulated philosophically in different ways, primarily by the Frankfurt School and by Habermas.

As we shall see in the next chapter, Foucault's challenge to Kantian anthropologism leads to a rather different philosophical outlook than the one promoted by Habermas. But it is in his monumental unfinished history of sexuality that this philosophical difference becomes more concrete; it involves a different idea of a critical theory than the one that Habermas has helped to make philosophically familiar.

In the work of Habermas, Bubner discerns an uneasy if not incoherent alliance between two distinct forms of critique, one Hegelian, the other Kantian.[2] Both Kantian and Hegelian critique, however, assume the philosophical humanism Foucault wants to challenge: he denies any foundational assumptions about our nature, and rejects the speculative theme of history as the self-realization of humanity. That is why in Foucault we find no "reconstruction" of Marx, no discussion of the "emancipatory potential" of the Communist Party, no socialist utopia, no dream of a rational society. Foucault wants to set aside what in *The Order of Things* he called the "commingled promises of dialectic and anthropology," and so to devise a different kind of "critical theory." It is not Hegelian in that the realization of a rational society is not its aim; and it is not Kantian since it is neither normative nor universalist.

In his inaugural lecture, Habermas argues that philosophy has been contemplative and theory has been traditional, since it has provided no way of realizing its ideals. Critical theory attempts to realize what traditional philosophy only "anticipates." The solution to the impasses of traditional philosophy is to reinterpret its ideals as an anticipation of a society that might be brought about through history. Thus Marxism reconstructed as a "critical theory" is a practice to realize universal enlightenment, and psychoanalysis a theory to realize genuine autonomy. Habermas finds in the very nature of human communication the ideals which philosophy has anticipated and which it is the task of a critical theory to help mankind accept.[3] Critical theory is thus a theory with this "practical intent."

Foucault's use of theory in critical struggles does not conform to this general model. Habermas starts with the assumption that philosophy has articulated the ideals critical theory must make practical. Foucault starts with the assumption that ideals and norms are always already "practical"; the point of critique is to analyze the practices in which those norms actually figure, and which determine particular kinds of experience. Norms are not in need of a practice; they are already elements in a complex which it is the task of critical thought to expose. In thus assuming that theories *are* practices, Foucault transforms the traditional relation of theory *to* practice found in the distinctions ideal/material and constitutive/regulative.

The central issue in his critique is neither the justification nor the realization of philosophical ideals of communication; it is the willingness or the unwillingness of people to play their roles in specific though anonymous configurations of power. In his conception, critique would increase the estrangement with which people participate in such configurations, but would not supply them with another form of life more in accord with philosophical principles. Thus he does not advance a global critique of all of society and its political institutions by reference to the standards of an ideal form of life. Rather he directs his "criticial theory" to those historical forms of experience whose "politics" no state or society can easily ignore.

The Professor-Critic

Freud and Marx provided Habermas with the instances of what he calls a critical theory. He "reconstructs" both in terms of the general image of a *Bildungsprozess* through which history overcomes dogmatism and irrationality; he argues that critical theory is "practical" because it enlightens through emancipation and emancipates through enlightenment. Thus Habermas justifies the familiar figure of the professor-critic who carries forth the process of historical enlightenment by helping society to reflect on its grounds, by determining the foundations of knowledge, by mercilessly exposing the philosophical deceptions of colleagues, raising the consciousness of students, and ferreting out the mystifications of previous generations. Foucault is somewhat suspicious of this figure—of what MacIntyre calls the "ideological self-righteousness"[4] of the Marxist critic as well as the "self-knowledge" of the enlightened Freudian.

In fact, Foucault attempts to develop a kind of critique which is precisely *not* patterned on the politics of a communist party or on the procedures of a psychoanalytic cure. He presents a different picture of the "politics" of critical struggles than the one the Marxist and Freudian models have determined. In particular, he questions the model of inverted enlightenment Geuss takes to be definitive of the very idea of a "critical theory."[5] In this model, ideology is the systematic prevention of free dialogue in which unreason and unfreedom are always implied by each other, and in which oppression therefore always "harbors" the possibility of a rational emancipation.

Foucault's suspicions about the professor-critic are supported by his challenge to these assumptions about critique. In his analysis, domination is not based on a refusal of reason and is quite compatible with truths about ourselves. He introduces a politics not simply of mystified consciousness but of the very forms of knowledge, and a critique that is not based on uncovering the emancipatory truth about our nature and our role in History.

Schooling Our Interests

In defining the nature of critical theory, Habermas makes use of the speculative theme of the systematic unity of knowledge. He postulates knowledge-constituting or cognitive Interests. He argues that the human race has basic interests and that those interests exactly match a division of inquiry that has its unity and basis in reason itself. There are two "lower interests" which correspond to the traditional distinction between *Naturwissenschaft* and *Geisteswissenschaft,* between natural and human science. Mankind has a different sort of interest in each kind of *Wissenschaft,* the interest in explaining and the interest in understanding. But man is also interested in emancipation or in becoming *mundig:* mature, major, responsible.

The postulation of this third and higher interest is the basic point of Habermas' classification. He finds it in the philosophical struggle against dogmatism and false authority exemplified in Kant and Fichte. But it is continued in what he calls the "critical theory" of Marx and Freud. Thus he uses the postulated third interest to dispute the "positivistic self-misunderstanding" of Marx and Freud and what he sees as its dire historical consequences. Foucault also tries to analyze and question the claims to truth in Marxism and psychoanalysis, but it is not through a constitutive scheme of anthropological interests.

Such a classificatory scheme can be found in the plan of the nineteenth-century German university. Habermas, of course, holds that the interests derive from "the history of the human race comprehended as a self-formative process (*Bildungsprozess*)."[6] But the result is to make his scheme of the unity of reason seem like a vast projection of the university onto the educational processes of the species, as though the human race were obtaining its degree in *Mundigkeit* in some great University without walls. The "faculties" of this University would be the Interests of Man, and the requirements for graduation would be to overcome all dogmatism and illegitimate authority. The point of the projection would be to identify the Marxist transformation of society with the realization of Reason. Habermas would make the unity of human knowledge "practical" by transferring it from the University to the Party, and so would introduce a variant on the typical utopian theme of a society for and by the School.[7]

In Foucault's politics of knowledge we find no such *kind* of critique. He rejects the theme of a systematic unity of knowledge, and, therefore, the very idea of trying to make it "practical." He holds there is nothing deep-seated or anthropological about forms of inquiry or university curricula, much less about the "interests" of communist parties. Like Nietzsche, he has no use for the division of knowledge into faculties. A complex history of changing practices is what has constituted the various disciplines and not the nature of man and his interests.

Foucault's theory of knowledge is filled with reference to aims or interests. But his point in referring to them is not to provide a fixed framework of inquiry, or to find its sources in our nature. For Foucault there *are* interests in knowledge but they are not "quasi-transcendental" ones. They are humble, practical, and changeable. They are discovered through historical research rather than through philosophical reflection on man.

Thus he finds interests which do not fit into Habermas' "faculties" and sciences in his faculties which do not have the interests he attributes to them. In social science, the aims are not exhausted by prediction, understanding, and emancipation. Foucault finds rather the aim of disciplining the body, normalizing behavior, administering the life of populations. He finds the aim of inserting people, or inducing them to insert themselves, into systems of categories and procedures of self-description through which they become governable.

Habermas thinks that when social scientists measure they have the interest in explaining, but when they talk with their subjects, they have the interest in understanding. Foucault's analysis of the counting practices, which overtook the social sciences in the nineteenth century, finds another aim: the control of deviancy.[8] In "dialoguing" with their patients, the nineteenth-century doctors of deviancy were not departing from this aim. Both dialogue and measurement figured in a historical practice with an aim for which Habermas' division of human faculties has no place.

This difference between historical aims and "constitutive" interests, of course, also applies to the sciences of psychoanalysis and historical materialism. Philosophical reflection may convince us that these sciences answer to our basic interest in autonomy. But the knowledge about "labor" and about "interaction" may have other aims than the transformation of nature and the institution of free and open talk. To find those aims, philosophical or anthropological reflection is not enough; we must examine the workings of actual practices.

There is a general difference between Foucault's humble historical aims and Habermas' knowledge-constitutive interests. The historical aims of bodies of knowledge can be criticized and changed; the "quasi-transcendental" aspects of ourselves to which Habermas refers cannot. This difference reflects a larger divergence in critical theory. In referring to the aims of knowledge, Foucault is not attempting to supply critique with a position in the university or in universal history; he does not think it needs a place in a master scheme or a historical teleology. Foucault is said to oppose Enlightenment itself. What he does question is the idealist picture of enlightenment as the historical formation of the species toward an ideal state. For Foucault, the truth of critique is not final; it is something that must always be taken up anew.

Liberation Politics

In reflecting on sexuality as a historical object, Foucault sought to expand the field of sexual politics and to question some of its basic models. Since Reich and Marcuse, critical history of sexuality had been oriented to determining the sources of repression in the family and thus of determining the conditions for a nonrepressive society. The focus was on the blocking of the natural expression of sexuality and its consequences for individual autonomy. The blocking of sexuality would occur primarily in the family, but, more generally, in any "authoritarian" institution. Liberation would lie in a release of sexuality from authoritarian restraint, or in the acquisition of "adult" relations among autonomous subjects. In short, the central aim of sexual politics was to overcome sexual denial in the family and thus free us for public life.

Foucault wants to suggest that sexual politics is much *more* than this.[9] He focuses on the constitution of subjectivity in specific historical forms of sexual experience rather than on the problem of the blocking of instincts and the unfreedom it instills. His question is how people become subject to a particular kind of sexual experience, supported by forms of knowledge, systems of constraint, and conceptions of human nature: "How an 'experience' was constituted such that individuals were to recognize themselves as subjects of a sexuality which opened onto very diverse domains of knowledge, and which was articulated on a system of rules and constraints."[10]

In orienting his critical history to this question, Foucault distances himself from the Reich-Marcuse model. He proposes a picture of domination not based on the paternal authoritarianism or the repression of instincts; a critical analysis which does not assume the form of discovering the truth about our repressed desires, and a concept of liberation or freedom which does not consist in the release of those desires from repression. Thus he attempts to devise a new kind of critique which would no longer be based on traditional models of alienation, mystification, and repression.

The Model of Alienation

Foucault's analysis of discipline was an analysis of objectification—of procedures which take us as objects and which involve us in relations of domination. But he does not take objectification as a suppression of rational dialogue, or of the true interests such dialogue might discover. Objectification is much more than a suppression of enlightened discussion. "The processes of objectification originate in the very tactics of power and the arrangement of its exercise."[11] They do not originate in alienation of an ideal intersubjectivity.

When, therefore, Foucault turns to the political problem of subjectivity in his *History of Sexuality*, it is not in terms of the ideal autonomy the processes of objectification are presumed to "alienate." Subjectivity is political for Foucault rather because of concrete procedures of "subjectivization—procedures through which we come to recognize ourselves as subjects of a form of experience which rests on a body of knowledge, norms, and models of our nature. Foucault's politics of subjectivity does not start with an ideal autonomy as a standard of critique, but with an analysis of the historical forms of the constitution of the subject.

Since he thus proposes to analyze the "tactics" of both objectification and subjectification in terms of actual identifiable practices, his critique abandons the supposed "dialectical" relation between subject and object which is the basis of the model of alienation. Negation does not figure as a category in his analysis.[12]

The Model of Ideological Mystification

In the traditional model, critique is focused on ideology. Ideology is the body of irrational belief that stands between us and our "enlightened" or true interests. It is a form of power or domination which is not violent or based on force, but which prevents us from freely pursuing those interests. To demystify an ideology is therefore to discover our true interests and assume our role in history. Habermas gives a strong normative reading of "irrational" on the Kantian model that identifies "morally right" with "justified to any rational agent." Ideology is "irrational" in that it prevents us from realizing the society based on rational assent among autonomous agents.

Foucault moves away from this model in either its historical or its normative Kantian form. In *Discipline and Punish,* he advances a critique which is not focused on ideology and which does not seek to provide access to our role in History. In his history of sexual morality, he questions the aim of inducing rational assent to sexual norms. He examines the kinds of sexuality which the attempts to fix universal norms have presupposed (such as stoical conceptions of conjugal duties).

Generally, there is a progressively pronounced departure from ideology as the focus of critique in Foucault's work, and a move toward a minute analysis of the practices that make particular forms of experience historically possible. Thus one point of analyzing knowledge as a "discursive practice" in *The Archaeology of Knowledge* was to avoid the Althusserian distinction between ideology and science; and one consequence of the analysis of discipline as a group of practices that target the body was to question the traditional Marxist dichotomy between ideology and violence (or between "external" and "internal" domination).

In *Discipline and Punish,* he argues that power gets its grip on us in much more direct and concrete ways than through the simple inculcation of irrational beliefs; it is directed at the very formation of our bodies and our identities. To reduce all nonviolent domination to ideology is to introduce a restrictive picture of its operations. It is a privative or negative picture, unspecific or abstract. It understands the exercise or "tactics" of domination in terms of something they must prevent (such as rational public consensus) or something they must frustrate (such as the fully enlightened pursuit of interest) rather than in terms of actual tangible procedures that determine the forms of experience in which we find ourselves. It singles out only one kind of power, and it turns the central issue in the analysis of power into a problem about the falsification of our true nature, taken as an abstract given.

Accordingly, Foucault's critical history of sexuality does not take "ideologies of sexuality" as its object. Rather it assumes the form of what he was already calling, in the last

pages of *The Archaeology of Knowledge,* an "archeology of the
ethical": an analysis of the way norms have figured in larger
"discursive practices" which supply a time and a place with a
particular framework of possible action and thought; an attempt to understand sex morals in terms of a larger unnoticed
"ethic" analyzed in terms of practices with different sources
and institutional implantations.

    Much as "discourse" for Foucault is not a lore of
belief that might be held as a coherent whole by a single infor-
mant, but is many people talking at once in conflicting ways, so
a "practice" is a body of discourse and procedure, which has
roots in different places and communities, which comprises
differences in opinion and in institutional application, which is
not planned, directed, or "owned" by anyone, and which has
unforeseen consequences.[13] Like "discourses," Foucault takes
"practices" to be anonymous and relatively autonomous. He
tries to analyze how norms become effective in practices of this
sort, and so acquire results unlike those that normative reflection might associate with them.

    A "discursive practice" is therefore not the self-
conscious activity of a moral community. It does not cover a
"life-world" which might be made fully rational by inducing
everyone to agree to its principles. Norms do not figure in
discursive practices as governing principles which members of
the community reflexively abstract and evaluate. The critical
analysis of a discursive practice is therefore not an attempt to
rationalize morals or to overcome ideological "irrationality."

    A central argument in volumes 2 and 3 of the
History of Sexuality is that norms of sexual austerity have had a
much longer continuity in our civilization than is often supposed. On the other hand, there has been considerable varia-
tion in the kinds of practices and, therefore, in the kinds
of experience or ethic in which such norms have figured.
Foucault's history is about those variations. He argues that
norms of sexual austerity have a different role in the Greek
regime of *aphrodisia* with its virile conception and its problem
of loving noble boys, than they do in the Christian regime of
the flesh with its problem of the submission of each soul to

ungodly or sinful thoughts. Foucault analyzes the "discursive practices" which account for such differences in the "experience of sexuality." He thus introduces a new sort of critical question.

His critical question is not the principled acceptance or rejection of moral codes; that is part of his object. He does not attempt to discover our true interests or the norms we must all, if we are not "irrational," agree to obey. He asks not how to make our sexual experience "rational," but whether we can have, and indeed whether we in fact want, another kind of "experience of sexuality" than the one which our practices make possible—another kind of sexual "ethic."

An "ethic" of sexuality is not a morality; it is the constitution of a form of experience through a complex of very diverse practices. An "archaeology" of those practices does not have a justificatory aim. It is an ethical critique whose basic issue is not the justification of norms to autonomous rational agents.

In short, Foucault does not look beyond or behind historical practices for the final truths about our nature or the norms our reason dictates to us. He attempts to look more closely *at* the workings of those practices in which moral norms and truths about ourselves figure, and to submit *them* to a critical analysis. Thus he questions the centrality of the model of ideology in critique; he questions the assumption that power works primarily through a mystification or falsification of a true, or rationally grounded, experience.

The Model of Repression

The Reich-Marcuse model of repression combines the models of alienation and mystification. It starts with the assumption that a basic misunderstanding of sexual desires (mystification) is at the root of our failure to achieve genuine autonomy (alienation). To undo repression through self-criticism (demystification) is thus to discover the truth about our desires that we must know in order to be free (disalienation).

We have seen that Foucault raises a common sort of objection against the models of alienation and ideology in critique: he questions starting critique with an anthropological given, a postulated truth about ourselves, which counterfactually conditions domination and so must emerge when domination is undone. Thus he also challenges the repression model. Instead of starting with our conception of sexuality taken as a given, he attempts to uncover other kinds of sexuality in different times and places. Instead of assuming that our true desires are the counterfactual condition of repression, he asks how a conception of "true desires"—repressed or otherwise—become part of *our* kind of sexuality.

Part of the objection to the "repressive hypothesis," with which he introduces his *History of Sexuality*, is that it leads to questionable historical assumptions. It does not seem to be the case that actual interdictions of sexual activity have always led to the kinds of elaborate misunderstanding of desires that the model of repression would have us suppose. We do, of course, find a pattern of thought and custom that disqualifies sex when it is not reduced to legitimate, reproductive acts. But this pattern is not the invention of capitalism or Christianity; it occurs earlier and elsewhere. Where we do find it, moreover, the areas of sexual experience which were taken to be morally problematic were often precisely areas in which sexuality was *not* forbidden or subject to interdiction. For such reasons, the repression model is misleading as a general historical hypothesis.

But Foucault also raises ethical or political objections to the model. It has introduced a misleading image of liberation; in setting the goal of removing repression through a great social transformation, it has directed us to misguided sorts of critical question. We can see this in relation to Habermas.

Habermas argues that it is precisely because the Freudian model of repression entails alienation and mystification that it provides us with the very model of a "critical theory." He claims that psychoanalysis provides the "only tangible example" of the "new kind of theory" which attempts to make Reason practical.[14] In psychoanalysis, theory has a "practical intent": to free oneself one must know the truth about oneself, and to know this truth *is* to free oneself. Self-knowledge and self-transformation imply one another. Psychoanalysis is therefore a theory whose truth or acceptance depends in part on such a "practical" enlightenment.

Habermas proposes an Idealist reading of Freud that interprets repression as alienation and privatization. He sees Freud as making a contribution to the "universal pragmatics" of communication. He "reconstructs" Freudian therapy as a sort of dialogic reeducation of the will to autonomy. Three theses can be distinguished. The first thesis is that therapy frees just what repression keeps from discussion. Though the source of repression is a faulty upbringing or *Bildung*, its result is to prevent one from being able to be truthful (*wahrhaftig*) in dialogue. Learning to be truthful in analysis is thus a "compensatory self-formation (*Bildungsprozess*)" that undoes repression. Since being truthful is incompatible with being repressed, in learning to be truthful, one undoes the self-imposed unfreedom one's unfortunate formation has induced. The second thesis (even less evident in Freud) consists in associating this freedom in truthful dialogue with "publicness, which means communicability in words and actions."[15] Therapy makes public and communicable what repression has privatized. To reeducate the will is to place one's actions under the light of public meanings and conventions. Combining the two theses, we can say: to learn to be truthful in dialogue is to make everything one says and does publicly communicable. The third thesis (which Freud denied) is that the basic repression which keeps one's thoughts and actions from being publicly communicable is "the result of suppression by social institutions."[16] Thus we can envisage the "nonrepressive society." It is the one whose *Bildung* does not suppress, but rather forms a public in which everyone can be truthful in dialogue, in which there are no "split-off" or "privatized" symbols in anything said or done, in which the desires of each are communicable to all. It is the society of "universally practiced dialogue." It is the "emancipated society whose member's *Mundigkeit* has been realized."[17]

There have been a number of objections to this discussion of psychoanalysis: questions about the account of Freud, about the advisability of transferring therapeutic models to social analysis, and about the plausibility of assimilating therapeutic self-reflection with the idealist reflection on the conditions of knowledge and morality. Foucault implicitly challenges the very idea that Freud "reconstructed" in this way provides a good model for critical theory.

Habermas' appropriation of psychoanalysis is historical only in that it is utopian. He sees psychoanalysis as the invention of a single man who unknowingly extended an idealist tradition descending from Kant. He reads Freud in terms of a "universal pragmatics" of speech which he then offers as a normative principle for the realization of the "non-repressive" or rational society. It is thus the utopian implications of Freud that make his work historically significant.

Foucault uses history in another way. He does not start with a utopian or normative "reconstruction" of Freudian models, but with a kind of practical and historical doubt about their use: he starts with the suggestion that there may be more to the historical determination of sexual desire than the prevention of our capacity to publicly formulate it. Thus his critique does not start with the question of what, in our language, allows us to envisage a society in which the irrationalities of sex would be abolished, but what, in our actual use of language or discourse, helps to determine our experience of sexuality.

In the second place, instead of taking knowledge of our "true desires" as a counterfactual condition of critique, Foucault takes it as one of its *objects:* he argues that psychoanalysis is hardly the first or the "only tangible" instance of a theory about the self which, when applied by an individual to himself, leads him to a truth he must know in order to be free. There is a long continuity in such theories, starting with the Greeks and exemplified notably by Christian practices of confession. A complicated if unnoticed history stands behind a "theory with a practical intent," a theory "addressed" to those presumed to suffer from irrational self-imposed constraints, who are thus in need of meticulous self-examination—those whose deficient public performance is rooted in an inability to formulate a truth about sexuality before a specially trained listener. Our nineteenth-century doctors of deviancy were rife with such "practical intentions"; one can even find the focus on the family as the source of such dangerous untruth.

Foucault uses history to identify ordinary if tacit aims which underlie such "practical intent," rather than singling out Freud's role in a universal history in which larger, deeply-rooted "emancipatory" aims come to be realized or made practical.

In these ways Foucault turns the question of repression around. He does not ask how our sexual desires incurred an alienation and a mystification; he asks how practices to discover the truth about ourselves ever became part of our experience of sexuality. He asks what, in our historical experience of sex, has caused us to assume that there is a hidden truth about desires which we must formulate and express to others if we are to be free. He starts with no anthropological given about sexuality. He turns the problem about knowing the truth about our sexual desires from a condition of emancipation to an object of investigation.

Critical Philosophy

In questioning the uncritical reliance on the model of repression in sexual politics, Foucault develops his own sort of "critical theory": a form of critical analysis consistent with his rejection of philosophical anthropologism. It is distinctive in its appeal to a "practical" rather than an "ideal" freedom.

In Foucault's critique, freedom is not an ideal we must make practical. It is *already* practical; indeed it is extremely concrete. It resides in who is willing to do what in concrete situations of power. It is rooted not in autonomy or the capacity to determine actions according to rules all must rationally accept, but rather in the unwillingness to comply, the refusal to acquiesce, to fit ourselves in the practices through which we understand and rule ourselves and each other. Such noncompliance in concrete situations of power is not something we can abstract and institute in a new form of life. It is specific and unpredictable, not universal and grounded. Foucault thinks freedom should not be analyzed as an ideal form of life, just as domination should not be analyzed as what prevents the realization of such a life. Thus his critique is designed to sharpen revolt but not to institute a new society.

Foucault attempts to purge from his critical analysis an anthropologism and a historicism he associates with Idealist philosophy. He questions the very assumptions in Marx and Freud for which Habermas traces a heritage in Kant, Fichte, and Hegel. And yet he is not claiming that nothing good has come from Marx and Freud; without them his own kind of critique would not have been possible. In some sense, Marx and Freud were not only engaged in critique; they have determined our very picture of it. The difficulty with underwriting their achievements with Idealist or anthropological-historical assumptions is that it presents those achievements in a fixed, final, "founded" form. It protects *them* from rethinking and change. It turns what was once "critical" in their work into a kind of norm or law—a final truth, a final emancipation. For Foucault that is just what critical "truth" *cannot* be.

We must question practices of objectification and mystification. But we must also question the "politics of truth" in the very concept of critique that descends from Marx and Freud. Critique is also the constant submission of the "truth" of our thought to analysis. That obligation (and not the obligation to determine what, in our nature, grounds our experience) is at the heart of Foucault's conception of philosophy—of his attempt to replace an Idealist philosophy of final emancipation with a nominalist philosophy of endless revolt.

Notes

1. See "Subject and Power," in *Michel Foucault* (Chicago: Dreyfus and Rabinow, 1982), pp. 221–212. Foucault draws a distinction between his research and the attempt in the Frankfurt School "to investigate this kind of

rationalism which seems to be specific to our modern culture and which originates in *Aufklärung*"; he "would suggest another way of investigating the links between rationalization and power." In the next chapter I discuss why Foucault's analyses of "rationalization" are not a new version of the dialectic of Enlightenment; in this chapter I discuss how these analyses involve another kind of critical theory. Further remarks on this difference are to be found in *L'Impossible Prison,* esp. pp. 316ff.

2. Rüdiger Bubner, "Habermas' Concept of Critical Theory" in *Habermas: Critical Debates,* Thompson and Held, eds. (Cambridge: M.I.T. Press, 1982), pp. 42–57.

3. "From the beginning philosophy has presumed that the autonomy and responsibility (*Mundigkeit*) posited with the structure of language are not only anticipated but real . . . . Only when philosophy discovers in the dialectical course of history the traces of violence that deform repeated attempts at dialogue and recurrently close off the path to unconstrained communication does it further the process whose suspension it otherwise legitimates: mankind's evolution towards autonomy and responsibility." Jürgen Habermas, *Knowledge and Human Interests* (Boston: Beacon, 1971), pp. 314–315. Contrast Foucault, *Power/Knowledge,* p. 114: "Neither the dialectic, as logic of contradictions, nor semiotics, as the structure of communication, can account for the intrinsic intelligibility of conflicts. 'Dialectic' is a way of evading the always open and hazardous reality of conflict by reducing it to a Hegelian skeleton, and 'semiology' is a way of avoiding its violent, bloody and lethal character by reducing it to the calm Platonic form of language and dialogue." A central sense of *Mundigkeit* is the entitled emergence from tutelage as, for example, when Kant argues that a woman is always *unmundig* (under tutelage, incompetent to speak for herself) even if, when defending her husband in court, she can become rather *übermundig. Anthropology from a Pragmatic Point of View,* p. 79.

4. Alasdair MacIntyre, "Ideology, Social Science, and Revolution," *Comparative Politics* (1973), 5:322.

5. Raymond Geuss, *The Idea of a Critical Theory* (Cambridge: Cambridge University Press, 1981).

6. Habermas, *Knowledge and Human Interests,* p. 5.

7. On this point see Jean-François Lyotard, *La Condition postmoderne,* and Michèle le Dœuff, "Utopias: Scholarly," in *Social Research* (Summer 1982), vol. 49, no. 2.

8. For Habermas see *Theory and Practice,* p. 10.

9. In *Power/Knowledge,* p. 59, Foucault says "I would . . . distinguish myself from para-Marxists like Marcuse who give the notion of repression an exaggerated role—because power would be a fragile thing if its only function were to repress, if it worked only through the mode of censorship, exclusion, blockage and repression, in the manner of a great Superego, exercising itself only in a negative way." On this point see my "Analysis in Power," in *Semiotexte,* (1977), vol. 2, no. 3.

10. Foucault, *L'Usage des plaisirs,* p. 10.

11. *Discipline and Punish,* p. 201.

12. See note 3.

13. Cf. *L'Impossible Prison*, p. 36–37. In response to the objection that his conception of practice is anonymous and automatic, Foucault retorts what would a "strategy" be which was *not* "born from several ideas formulated and proposed from different points of view or objectives, . . . finds its motive in several results concurrently sought, with diverse obstacles to overcome, and different means to combine . . . which doesn't owe its value and its chances for success to a certain number of interests?" Foucault's "practice" is thus not Aristotle's *praxis:* there is a change in the *concept* of freedom in practices, not its elimination.

14. Habermas, *Knowledge and Human Interests,* p. 214.

15. *Ibid.,* p. 238.

16. *Ibid.,* p. 283. Habermas claims that Freud had not so much a theory of society as an ideal or utopia which might be used in a normative theory of society.

17. *Ibid.,* p. 314. Foucault wonders whether this would be such a desirable outcome.

CHAPTER FOUR

The Freedom of Philosophy

Philosopher-Intellectual

Foucault's "philosophy" is characterized by his attempts to rethink philosophical problems in terms of the aims and obligations of the engaged secular intellectual—of what he calls the "ethic of the intellectual." He was a philosopher-intellectual; the figure of his philosophy is not the scientist, the moralist, the sage, the priest, the writer, or artist, but the intellectual in his restless questioning of the social and artistic movements of his time.

In Britain, an intellectual tends to be a historian; in America, at least since the great period of pragmatism, a sociologist, political scientist, or literary critic. In France, however, following Sartre, he tends to be a philosopher. Husserl, Kierkegaard, Wittgenstein, and Quine may all be important modern philosophers; they are not "intellectuals" in the sense that an "ethic of the intellectual" is not placed at the center of their very conceptions of doing philosophy.

For Foucault, philosophy must matter to non-philosophers—to those whose profession is not philosophy. The *point* of doing philosophy is to occasion new ways of thinking about the forms of experience around which there exist controversy and protest. His philosophy is for those whose experience is problematized in his nominalist histories. One might even say that its basic principle is that the "truth" of those historical analyses lies in "freeing" new thinking—that is Foucault's way of transforming the relation between "truth" and "freedom" characteristic of our philosophical tradition.

Thus Foucault devises his own style of philosophy. It is controversial in several respects:

1. The basic aim of his philosophy is not professional; it goes beyond academic discussion. The way it goes beyond this discussion is not as a supervenient foundationalist enterprise: philosophy does not help to organize and evaluate other "faculties" of knowledge. On the contrary, it is the analysis of "external" problems which is used to challenge and rethink "philosophical" ones.[1]

2. It is not a programmatic philosophy, but instead makes a virtue of change, endless rethinking, fundamental questioning. Foucault's philosophy cannot be said to belong to any of the major "programs" which have dominated the field in our century: not the Fregean program many see Wittgenstein as transforming, not the phenomenological thought Husserl initiated and many see Heidegger as transforming; not the logical positivism politics chased from Vienna and which survived through its English-language qualifications and reformulations; not hermeneutics, not neo-Hegelian sociology or "communicative ethics." Foucault even denies he was a structuralist. He has not initiated a philosophical program; increasingly, his work becomes devoid of philosophical jargon, and no "ism" attaches to his name.

3. Foucault assumes that the "problems" of philosophy do not comprise an unchanging and autonomous corpus, but themselves undergo changes and have a history. To assert this, however, is not to reduce philosophical thought to intellectual history. It is not to revive the old theme of the "end of philosophy." It is to define a task of constantly rethinking of transforming the questions of philosophy in the light of those external problems toward which one's intellectual obligations direct one.

The thesis that philosophy has a history that matters to philosophical reflection itself is one that is generally rejected in mainstream analytic philosophy. Foucault finds it in Kant; Kant would initiate the obligation of philosophers to provide a kind of historical diagnosis for the thought of their day.[2] Both Hegel and Heidegger make the history of philosophy important to philosophy, but Foucault's use of history is not a simple continuation of either. It is not just that Foucault's historical research involves much more detailed attention to nonphilosophical and noncanonical works. It is not just that he rejects global schemes or narratives in which philosophy would figure as a culminating or irruptive point (he has no talk of the progress of reason in history, or the end of metaphysics). He forms a particular conception of what constitutes a philosophical tradition or what accounts for the emergence and transformation of philosophical problems.

Foucault's philosophical use of history is not an attempt to respond to a Heideggerian Destiny or to announce a great Hegelian moment in universal history. In fact he rejects the idea of universal history; his work is not about the destiny of Western thought. His histories are rather a series of discrete problematizations. They are precise little surgical operations that attempt to isolate a philosophical disease, to problematize the very terms in which a philosophical difficulty is raised. In this sense he resembles Wittgenstein; he uses historical research into the ancestries of our ways of thinking to show the fly the way out of the bottle.

He thinks it is vain to find the sources of our philosophical problems in the fundamental character of our nature, our reason, or our world. His conception of the history of philosophy makes no reference to such "foundations." Many divergent sources and circumstances have supplied philosophy with its questions and procedures; scientists, priests, moralists, and judges have all contributed. Philosophy is historical because it continues discussion among other people, talking back and forth in often antagonistic ways in lower and lesser places; without this more humble discussion it would not be possible at all. Desttut de Tracy is as essential a figure as Kant, and some forgotten police administrator may make a contribution to morals as essential as Hume's. To understand a philosophical problem is to discover the connections it has with such lowly discussion; that is how it acquires a history.

That history cannot therefore be discovered through an exclusive reliance on the constitution of canonical works and their interpretation. Philosophy is not an Olympian creation of a holistic canon for endless exegesis or dialogue; it has lowly origins and not noble ones like enraptured contemplation or disinterested arbitration. To understand its problems is to identify those sources. For this one cannot rely on such "unities" of philosophical commentary as the work, the author, or the genre, or even newer ones like research communities or disciplinary paradigms. Rather with one's scalpel one must cut out from the writings of philosophers or thinkers those elements that are implicated in the battles and debates in other quarters. The problem is not to reproduce a heritage, but to problematize a portion of our current thought by discovering its historical lineages.

Language is not a sufficient tool for identifying a tradition in philosophy, and one and the same tradition can be carried on in several languages at once. Language is not a good *model* for a philosophical tradition; Foucault has none of the metaphors of "dialogue" or what Gadamer calls the "linguisticality" of philosophical traditions. Philosophical problems are rather conflict, dilemma, and paradox.

History is not important to philosophy as a great narrative of the West into which one must fit one's thought. There are different sorts of philosophical problems, and they have different sorts of history. The philosopher uses history to find material roots, to diagnose, to reformulate, to problematize or to dissolve what he thus identifies as the philosophical problems of his time and situation. It is in terms of this conception of its history that Foucault attempts to define the role of philosophy in the ethic of the intellectual.

There are two basic questions to which Foucault applied this conception of the history of philosophy: the question of knowledge or science, and the question of the constitution of the subject. One objection he had to Sartre was that he provided no way of coming to terms with these questions—either intellectually or philosophically. They were Foucault's way out of the phenomenological and Marxist philosophy characteristic of postwar France.

More generally, Foucault holds that a basic division which runs throughout French philosophy since the introduction of Husserl in the thirties is the conflict between a "phenomenological" philosophy in which the subject is given a constitutive role and a philosophy of science in which that role is denied. Adopting a distinction made by Cavailles, the French philosopher of science, Foucault argues that there is a

> line which separates a philosophy of experience, meaning, and the subject from a philosophy of *savoir,* rationality, and the concept. On the one side, a filiation which is that of Sartre and Merleau-Ponty, and, on the other, one which is that of Cavailles, Bachelard, and Canguilhem. Alternatively, it is a matter of two modalities according to which phenomenology was taken up in France.[3]

The problems of the subject and of knowledge, central to this division, are the ones Foucault himself was to continuously rethink and interrelate. It would not be difficult to show that there has been philosophical controversy about these problems in all modern European languages and traditions. In attempting to work out their history, Foucault makes the distinctive assumption that the subject is not the condition of knowledge, but that knowledge about the subject is one of the historical forms through which subjective experience is constituted. The subject is not an invention of philosophy, but a historically constituted entity problematic enough to give rise to philosophical controversy. Foucault examines that history; he raises the problem of the subject in terms of the lowly practices and bodies of knowledge in which it figures.

He tries to show how developments in the way we conceive of our economy, language, and biology force on us a recognition of our finite nature; how new kinds of knowledge about our abnormalities require us to question our ideas about ourselves as autonomous agents; how the introduction of therapeutic forms of confession have induced in us beliefs about our unconscious selves; how sexuality became problematized through the procedures by which we constitute ourselves as moral subjects. Such lowly bodies of knowledge and practice in which our self-conceptions are rooted, are, for Foucault, a source of philosophical controversy about knowledge and the subject. In them the battle is carried on, which the philosophical debates continue and without which they would not be possible. To discover these sources is to alter our understanding of those debates.

In *The Order of Things,* Foucault declares that philosophical anthropology "constitutes perhaps the most fundamental arrangement that has governed and controlled the path of philosophical thought from Kant until our own day."[4] It amounts to our philosophical "slumber"; to think again we must awake from it. Such declarations earned Foucault a notoriety; he was hounded for the rest of his career for the suggestion that Man was a recent invention that might disappear. Yet he did not invent the problem; it was central to the philosophical discussion of his time. Rather he attempted to use history to ask how the problem arose: what was so problematic about the philosophical conception of Man that to announce his end should occasion such outcry?

In asking this question, Foucault sought to rethink the very aims of philosophy. For anthropology had helped to determine a link of philosophy to the University, by asking what in Man allows us to supply the unity and grounds of all the other disciplines. And it had contributed to the formulation of the intellectual task of assisting the historical realization of the essence of Man. In asking about the historical sources of anthropology, Foucault was thus questioning both the academic foundational model of philosophy, and the finalism of the ethic of human engagement.

Freedom was the concept Sartre placed at the center of his philosophy; it was the cardinal principle in his ethic of the intellectual. Foucault's philosophy, however, by historicizing the problems of knowledge and of the subject, introduces a new concept of freedom, and thus transforms the role of the philosopher-intellectual. It is the question of this freedom that is crucial in Foucault's philosophy. It is what is at issue in the storm of accusations of irrationalism, anarchism, and nihilism, which his philosophy has occasioned.

Kantian Questions

Kant defined the "problems of knowledge" for modern philosophy as a problem about the "conditions of the possibility" of knowledge. Foucault keeps much of this definition. He preserves the Kantian task of specifying the limits or bounds of possible objective thought, and the Kantian formulation of the nature of truth in terms of "constitution" rather than "correspondence." He asks how those domains are constituted in which objective discourse is possible. But he asks the question in a new way. He wants to "purge" this question "of all anthropologism" and raise it in terms of anonymous bodies of discourse. He wants to historicize it and turn it into a question about the emergence and transformation of such discourse. He wants to pluralize it and assume that there are different kinds or "regions" of objective knowledge, different "positivities." For each region of possible objective discourse, historical research is required to determine what constitutes its bounds.

In *The Order of Things* and *The Archaeology of Knowledge,* there is thus reference to a "historical *a priori,*" a deep organization of bodies of sentences of a particular time and place, which makes objective thought possible there and then. Foucault postulates a sort of transcendental realm which conditions knowledge but which is nonsubjective and changing. He introduces a picture of transcendence without a subject. In refocusing the Kantian questions in this way, he introduces a series of new philosophical problems: problems about reference and discontinuity, about realism, incommensurability, and change.

Thus one might say that Foucault invents a new historical way of doing Kantian philosophy of knowledge. And yet it is with quite peculiar intellectual aims. It is critical rather than foundational, and as much ethical as epistemological; it raises problems about *freedom* with respect to our participation in the realms that constitute knowledge. Foucault is a most paradoxical Kantian—one who has managed to gain notoriety as an irrationalist.

Foucault's philosophy of knowledge is as much ethical as epistemological since it is applied primarily to "moral sciences"—knowledge that is about us or that provides us with certain kinds of conceptions of ourselves. In particular it is applied to cases where the objectivity of knowledge raises ethical or political questions about our freedom.

We have seen such issues in his historical work, for example, in his analysis of the constitution of a science about mental illness. Political or ethical issues had been raised in the controversy over the medical objectification of madness. But they remained couched in an "anthropological" vocabulary about reification or alienation. Foucault was influenced by Althusser's attempts to weed out the Hegelian assumptions that vocabulary involves. He attempted to get rid of a series of metaphors. In being taken as objects of new forms of knowledge and practice such as psychiatry, it was not that our essence was somehow being entrapped, repressed, offended, or externalized. Rather, in being constituted as objects in such practice (as well as in cases where we constitute ourselves as subjects), we unwittingly participate in forms of domination. Thus our freedom does not lie in some nature that has been alienated in, and might be rescued from, such practice, but in our capacity to question the practices themselves. Anonymous objectivizing (and subjectivizing) forms of knowledge require from us a complex participation which we can contest and change. But in cases like mental illness, what makes knowledge "objective" (what secures reference to an object about which it is possible to have true and false discourse) is part of what makes it "objectivizing" (what links knowledge to techniques of domination).

Thus Foucault wants not only to "purge" epistemology of all "anthropologism," and to assert that no transcendental subject, individual or collective, provides the basis and grounds of knowledge. He also wants to so purge ethics and to assert that our freedom is found not in our transcendental nature but in our capacities to contest and change those anonymous practices that constitute our nature.

In the analytic tradition, the first sort of purgation is more palatable than the second. There are several mainstream positions which hold that "the mind" is not central to "epistemology," and which reject what Strawson called "the mythical subject of transcendental psychology." Indeed Frege is often credited with initiating the analytic paradigm, precisely by purging philosophy of "psychologism" and directing it toward a formal analysis of language and logic.

Unlike Foucault, however, analytic philosophers, in banishing "the mind" from epistemological reflection, have preserved Kant's basic intellectual purposes while abstracting them from ethical implications. No one, after all, is surprised to encounter the Kantian subject in *moral* philosophy; no one complains about the "mythical subject of transcendental psychology" in Rawls' discussion about an original position in which subjects contract with each other without knowing who they are. Thus Foucault's ethical "purgation" of the subject, which finds freedom not in the mutual obligations of rational agents to obey universal moral laws, but in our real capacity to change the practices in which we are constituted or constitute ourselves as moral subjects, seems irrationalist even to those who share his desire to rid epistemology of the transcendental subject.

In the philosophy of science, even Popper postulates an impersonal realm where objective knowledge is made possible—the "third world," which can be reduced neither to the world of persons nor to the world of things. Foucault may provide a more "materialist" picture of the realm as comprised of actual documents rooted in specific institutional practices, but he shares the thesis that objectivity is secured in a nonsubjective world. In his attempts to provide a historical criterion for rationality, Lakatos adopts a similar position.

We can measure Foucault's distance from Popper or Lakatos by the changes he introduces into the focus, the aim, and the conception of the Kantian attempt to determine the bounds of objective discourse in impersonal terms. Through these changes he departs from the basic intellectual aim of securing rationality, which Popper and Lakatos inherit from Kant, and tries to replace it with another. These changes comprise his singularity as a Kantian.

First is *change in focus:* Foucault applies the Kantian questions not to established sciences like physics, but to what Ian Hacking calls "immature science"—knowledge in the "preparadigm" stage, not yet dominated by formal theory and more closely tied to external conditions.[5] He argues that different kinds of positivity, or different regions of objective discourse, raise different kinds of philosophical problems. He thus disputes the unity of science, or what he calls the "positivist hierarchy of science";

> the history of sciences concerned itself preferentially if not exclusively with a few noble disciplines, noble by the age of their foundation, their high degree of formalisation, by the privileged place they occupied in the positivist hierarchy of sciences. . . . The problem raised by the development of a science is not necessarily in direct proportion to the degree of formalisation it has attained . . . [there are] middle regions where knowledges are much less deductive, much more dependent on external processes, and where they remained much longer in thrall to the prestige of the imagination.[6]

Foucault's work is about knowledge in such "middle regions." It is about ignoble sciences like forensic psychiatry, where abstract formal theory does not command the pattern of development and where external processes are much more important. The problems he finds in the development of such sciences are thus different in kind from those that concern Popper and Lakatos. They are not problems about nomological-deductive inference or about theory appraisal. They are problems about our freedom, about our participation in practices that suppose forms of domination. They are problems not about unwarranted belief but about the acceptance of those practices which define us.

There is thus a *change in the aim* in asking Kantian questions about the bounds of objective discourse. Foucault's aim is not to provide a "demarcation criterion" or to determine when claims to objectivity are justified. In fact he examines sciences or bodies of knowledge in which he himself does *not* believe or about which he is skeptical. It is precisely in such cases that he seeks to determine the bounds of objectivity. He is not attempting to define what warrants the assertability to bodies of knowledge like psychiatry, but to determine the historical contingency of its objects—to de-realize or "nominalize" them.

Finally there is *a change in what counts as the bounds of objective discourse.* The bounds of objective discourse in immature science are found not in the justification of methods but in the constitution of an object. Foucault's criticism of social science is distinguished by the fact that its angle of attack is one not of *methods* but of *objects;* there is little about the "positivism dispute" or about the old contrast between explanation and understanding. Thus, for example, the question as to what secures objective reference to "mental illness" is not a question about formal methods or theory justification, but about a complex of practice that determines the domain in which objective knowledge can occur.

It is this change in focus, aim, and conception that places Foucault's Kantian questions in a new intellectual frame. He is not asking in which kinds of discourse we are entitled to believe, but which kinds of practices tied to which kinds of external conditions determine the immature knowledge in which we ourselves figure. He wants to introduce a sense of contingency about those practices, to question the realism of their objects. Because there is no place for such aims within the tradition of Kantian rationalism, in Popper or in Lakatos, Foucault's philosophy has been called irrationalist. In fact it is about a new kind of problem, a problem about freedom.

Foucault's Kantian questions depart from the general intellectual project of defending the rational procedures of science and of weeding out prejudice and superstition. He seems to think that sciences like physics are no longer in need of a "philosophical" defense, and that there is something *dérisoire* in the attempts of philosophers to instruct scientists about theory appraisal. Philosophical reflection is needed rather in thinking about the new kinds of problems the emergence of the social sciences has raised.

In defining this new role for philosophy, he departs from Kantian rationalism in two ways:

1. Since there are many different sorts or regions of objective discourse, we need not assume that they are all supported or "grounded" in a single conception of Reason. To give up the philosophical conception of Reason as ground of knowledge, however, is not at all to loose all capacity for rational thought; it is, on the contrary, to extend it. We can grant the importance of critical standards and yet recognize that for a whole range of knowledge about ourselves and our societies, the possibility of objective knowledge is part of a practice that requires a tacit acceptance we can analyze and challenge.

2. Philosophies that defend Reason have had at least one role in defining our task as intellectuals which we need to question: their role in fabricating scientific utopias or dreams of a rational society, and in the invention of a "revolutionary" intellectual who would assist in the realization of such dreams. Foucault's philosophy is an attempt to distance us from that model of Reason; his analysis of social science is an attempt to expose its roots.

In elaborating this new role for Kantian questions, Foucault moves from an "archaeological" to a "genealogical" analysis of the ways in which the subject has been constituted in bodies of knowledge, forms of domination, and in the prescribed assumption of ethical codes.

Phenomenological Finitudes

The Order of Things was Foucault's attempt to dissolve the "anthropologism" in contemporary philosophy by providing an archaeology of its sources. It was a critical inquiry into how "reflections on subjectivity, the human being and finitude" had come to appropriate the very "value and function of philosophy." It was an argument for "anti-humanism" or the rejection of Man as a basic or foundational principle that governs or grounds all phenomena.

But it was an argument of a particular kind. "Archaeology" and "genealogy" both name strategies Foucault devises for using historical research to undercut foundational humanism. They supply his arguments to dissolve anthropologism; they are his active historical way of doing anti-humanist philosophy. But in moving from the first to the second, Foucault defines a distinctive political sort of anti-humanism.

In the late Heidegger and in Althusser's Marx, we also find a rejection of the foundational role of Man, an attempt to place the constitution of the subject in a historical framework, and a formulation of a new philosophy purged of humanism. Foucault's archaeologies and genealogies may thus be said to belong to this philosophical tradition. But as he turns to genealogy, Foucault raises objections to Althusser's conception of "ideology" as the framework in which the subject is constituted, and he replaces Heidegger's turn to "poetical thought" with a new politics. The germs of Foucault's "political anti-humanism" are, however, already to be found in the archaeological arguments of *The Order of Things;* they can be found in his attempt to unravel how the problem of knowledge had come to be formulated in terms of man's constitutive finitude.

In modern French and German philosophy, Kant's questions about the bounds of knowledge had been reformulated as problems about the nature of consciousness or existence, rather than as problems about logic and language. In his early work, Heidegger had attempted to turn man's "finite existence" into a fundamental or foundational phenomenon, and to turn philosophy into the analysis of that transcendental existence. All phenomena were to be interpreted in terms of their rootedness in man's existence and its basic structures.

In his 1929 *Kant and the Problem of Metaphysics,* Heidegger read his conception of a foundational finitude into Kant, and so attempted to "repeat" Kant's "question of the laying of the foundation of metaphysics." He refers to Kant's fourth question in his lectures on logic, the question "What is

Man?," which, Kant remarks, is the basis for the rest of his philosophy. Heidegger interprets that basic question as the "interrogation of the finitude of man." He moves from Kant's question about the limits of knowledge to a question about the nature of the being who can pose such questions. Thus he finds the possibility of the Kantian questions in our "finite existence"; we would "be there" to ask questions about the limits of our reason and our freedom.

In *The Order of Things,* Foucault also takes Kant's fourth question "What is Man?" as initiating an anthropological turn in philosophy. It is the begining of the attempts to find in man's "finite existence" the foundations of all knowledge. Rather than "repeating" this question, however, Foucault looks for its sources in the archaeology of knowledge. Those sources are more humble than anything the "high-minded few" concerned with the modern form of anthropological reflection would allow; they are "more prosaic and less moral." They also demonstrate how misguided that reflection is. Foucault argues that Kant's question "What is Man?" in fact "produces the confusion of the empirical and the transcendental even though Kant had demonstrated the division between them."[7]

He attempts to show that the displacement in transcendental reflection, from a model of "ideas" as representations of things unified in a *cogito,* to a model of the structures of man's "existence" in the world, matches and is made possible by an archaeological shift in the modes of knowledge about us.

"Finitude" emerges as an archaeological characteristic of the human sciences when the modern arrangement of knowledge about life, labor, and language is contrasted with the classical one. We then see how it was "heralded . . . in the positivity of knowledge" (p. 313); we then learn that it is "designated . . . on the basis of the empirical forms that can be assigned to (man's) existence . . . man assignable in his corporeal, laboring, speaking existence" (p. 318), and so realize how misguided it is to use such empirical forms to provide an *a priori* foundation for knowledge.

We "moderns" must regard ourselves as possessed of a "specific nature" which limits anything we can say or do.

Our language limits our thinking, our labor limits our wealth and our happiness, our life limits our actions and our wills, and so we become constituted as "finite" beings: speakers, workers, and organisms. In the preceding "classical" arrangement of the same domains, we figured as those beings who stand apart and represent their world to themselves without having a *specific* place within it. We could not be conceived as those beings whose specific "existence" is problematic. Thus in the practice of drawing up great classificatory tables characteristic of the classical arrangement of knowledge "the personage for whom the representation exists and who represents himself within it . . . is never found in that table himself" (p. 308).

The "I" does not appear in the table; it does not have a "nature" specific to it, and therefore it *cannot* have a "problem of existence." The "I exist" is reduced to the "I think"; the idea of "founding" knowledge in man's "existence" occurs to no one. It is thus only when the representational mode of knowledge lost its grip or its "power" on us, that a philosophical anthropology could arise.

> Anthropology as an analytic of man . . . became necessary at the moment when representation lost the power to determine . . . the interplay of its syntheses and analyses. It was necessary for empirical syntheses to be performed elsewhere than within the sovereignty of the "I think." They had to be required at precisely the point at which that sovereignty reached its limit, that is, in man's finitude—a finitude that is as much that of consciousness as that of the living, speaking, laboring individual. This had already been formulated by Kant in his *Logic*. (pp. 340–341)

Though finitude derives from new kinds of empirical knowledge, it is used to provide *a priori* foundations for all knowledge. There arises the peculiar and hopeless "attempt to make the man of nature, of exchange or of discourse, serve as the foundation of his own finitude" (p. 318). Man becomes at once empirical and transcendental, ontic and ontological. In this "doubling" there is a basic problem: empirical "forms of existence" are being used to provide the grounds of all knowledge. The "transcendental-empirical doublet" that results is a "strange figure," since "he is a being such that knowledge will be attained in him of what makes all knowledge possible" (p. 318). Looked at archaeologically, foundational anthropology is thus the impossible attempt "to give empirical contents transcendental value or to displace them in the directions of a constituent subjectivity" (p. 248).

Foucault's "archaeological" argument in *The Order of Things* thus has the following form: (1) a denial that the conditions of knowledge can be found in a reflection on man's finitude any more than they can be deduced from the "I think." The conditions of knowledge are found in the emergence and transformations of anonymous bodies of discourse; (2) since those conditions are historically contingent, it is vain to attempt to provide them with a philosophical "foundation" or "ground;" (3) the turn to "finite existence" as the object of foundational reflection is in fact made possible by a "more prosaic" historical change in the way we figure in the knowledge about us; (4) foundational analysis of our finite existence thus inherits or "repeats" the basic problem in post-Kantian though, the problem of a "transcendental-empirical" doubling, or the attempt to "give empirical contents transcendental value."

Philosophy should therefore give up the conception of a transcendental nature and the attempt to find the conditions of knowledge in it. Rather than attempting to provide an analysis for finitude, philosophy should ask through what historical practices "finitude" came to constitute a problem. Instead of being an occasion for fundamental ontology, finitude should be the starting point for a historical analysis. Instead of asking about our "fundamental" relation to "the world," "the body," "the other," and so forth, one should ask how those relations became problematic enough to require a philosophical analysis in the first place. Archaeology thus introduces a change in the role of philosophy—a critical and historical analysis of how we are involved in organizations of discourse that constitute us as "finite beings."

Following Heidegger, Gadamer tried to interpret finitude as situatedness in a tradition. Foucault interprets finitude as only a concept within a particular tradition, one that is problematized within a particular arrangement of knowledge. He thus introduces a different conception of a philosophical tradition, and a new role for philosophy: archaeological analysis, or the argument which, by placing the constitution of the subject within a humble or "prosaic" historical context, undercuts it as a foundation for knowledge, morals, or culture. The political point of such analysis is found in its "genealogical" version; as we shall see, it involves the concept of freedom, the concept Sartre had tried to turn into *the* philosophical and intellectual issue, through his appropriation of Heidegger's fundamental ontology.

In *The Order of Things,* we can already find an attempt to "de-anthropologize" the concept of freedom Sartre had used to define the role of the intellectual. For we can associate the shift in modes of knowledge with a corresponding shift in conceptions of freedom.

In the classical arrangement of knowledge one might say that we "freely" disposed of our representations of the world, and therefore of our actions within it. Our nature did not figure in that world as something that might limit our free capacity for representation. The legitimate state could be pictured as the self-representation of free subjects; the concept of self-legislation is not darkened by problems about our specific nature as speaking, living, working beings. There is no political problem about our constitution *as* subjects. There is no suspicion that our language, our work, and our bodies might determine the very description of our actions and our world in ways we don't realize and can't change.

In the classical era, the problem of the free will is a problem of initiating our representations from the *cogito,* and not a problem of projecting from the world into which we are thrown through our "original choices." When we acquire a finite nature, we acquire a new kind of moral and intellectual problem: we must *always* suspect that we are self-deceived, and that the true descriptions of what we do and think belong to an economic, linguistic, or biological order we systematically misunderstand. Our problem becomes "not the possibility of knowledge (*connaissance*) but the possibility of a primary misunderstanding (*méconnaissance*)" (p. 323). The anthropological turn in philosophy includes an anthropological definition of freedom, or an attempt to define it in terms of our finite nature, either as the limits if our nature which we must learn to "authentically" accept, or as the fundamental "alienation" of our nature we must overcome by transforming our entire society.

It thus defines new intellectual tasks which *The Order of Things* challenges in the discussion of the change in utopian thought. In the classical period, utopia was the dream of an ideal beginning in which everything would perfectly fit into the great Tables of Representation. In the nineteenth century it becomes a way of envisaging an end to history when our finitude would be expressed. Ricardo's "pessimism" and Marx's "revolutionary hope" are two versions of this attempt to understand history in terms of a constitutive finitude:

> The flow of development, with all its resources or drama, oblivion, alienation, will be held within an athropological finitude which finds in them, in turn, its own illuminated expression. *Finitude* with its truth is posited in *time,* and *time* is therefore *finite.* The great dream of an end to History is the utopia of causal systems of thought just as the dream of the world's beginnings was the utopia of the classifying systems of thought. (pp. 262–263)

In *The Order of Things,* Foucault wanted to "de-anthropologize" our nineteenth-century utopian imaginations, to dissociate our hopes from "realizing our essence," to separate our freedom from philosophical postulations about our nature. He opposes the theme of the end of history by uncovering its anthropological roots. He moves us from a Sartrian model of freedom as projection from the world, to a model of the historical problematization of the forms through which the conception of "our world" is given to us. This requires a *political* change which Nietzsche instigates. It is Nietzsche who "burns for us . . . the intermingled promises of the dialectic and anthropology" (p. 263).

Nietzsche's Politics

Foucault's 1970 paper on Nietzsche's conception of genealogy, as well as his own adoption of a "genealogical" strategy in historical research, occur during a period in which he attempts to rethink certain of his previous assumptions. He offers not simply a commentary of Nietzsche, he also *uses* Nietzsche to rethink and reformulate his own work. This use determines at least the focus of his commentary, and might even be counted as part of it. For in "doing" genealogy, Foucault exemplifies his conception of it.

There is a political core in the problems which led Foucault to his use/commentary of Nietzsche, which might be put by asking: what are the *politics* of the philosophical problematization of the subject; in what sense is anti-humanist philosophy of *political* importance for the engaged intellectual? Nietzsche assumes this political role for Foucault: in his "gay science" he turns the problem of knowledge into a problem about power, and in his historical analysis of "the will-to-knowledge," he offers a model for the political intellectual.

One can infer at least one strategy in Foucault's use/commentary of Nietzsche's genealogy: an attempt to "de-Nazify" his philosophy, and, in particular, his anti-humanism; to give it another kind of political interpretation. The great anti-humanist philosophers, Heidegger and Nietzsche, had both been used by Nazi ideologues, and Heidegger could hardly have been very inspiring to Foucault as a political intellectual. The anti-humanist strand in their thought was often condemned as a kind of totalitarian denial of individual freedom. Foucault makes Nietzsche into the philosopher of a new sort of freedom and a new sort of politics which can precisely *not* be the politics of a totalitarian state.

Within his Nietzschean or "genealogical" work, Foucault elaborates this conception of freedom—freedom not as the end of domination but as revolt within its practices, and domination not as repression or ideological mystification, but as dispersed formations of possible action which no one directs or controls. It is in this way that he devises a concept of political freedom within an anti-humanist framework. Heidegger's reflections on freedom had not resulted in a clear *political* conception; it is in his use/commentary of Nietzsche's genealogy that Foucault discovers one.

Henri Biraut presents a detailed case that Sartre had systematically misread Heidegger's thinking on freedom, when he interpreted it in terms of fundamental choice and project.[8] For the later Heidegger freedom is not subjective; it is the "clearing" of possibilities for thought and action in an epoch. In *The Order of Things,* Foucault is closer to Heidegger; his anti-humanism leads him along a similar path: the conception of an anonymous "emergence" or "appearance" of new possibilities of discourse, or new "positivities." His picture of the emergence of such regions of discourse matches with Heidegger's concept of the "clearing"; it is in the contingency of those bodies of discourse that Foucault also finds a source of freedom.

A problem *The Order of Things* thus shares with Heidegger is the political one of what to *do* about these configurations which freely "emerge" without choice or collective action. In Heidegger there are the attempts to recover a "pre-Socratic" thought and to find another and poetical kind of thinking. But Foucault wanted his anti-humanism to serve as a tool in his activities as a political intellectual. He wanted his archaeological or genealogical research to have a critical aim; to provide an analysis for the revolt and controversy surrounding the problem of subjectivity in our political and cultural life. He thus needed some way to make anti-humanism critical, to link the conception of freedom as historical contingency to something we can actually do, criticize, change.

The "archaeology of the human sciences" had remained rather abstract or uncertain as a form of political critique. To forecast that Man is about to disappear in the sands of discontinuity (even assuming it proved correct) was not a strong form of *criticism*. It suggests that there is nothing we can *do* about Man except to invent a whole new way of thinking and behaving in which Man would no longer have a fundamental role. In effect, the critical part of Foucault's reflections in that book is supported by rhetoric and narrative, by the image that we are living in some great irruptive moment in which all will be changed—and that is not much of a criticism. The movement from the archaeology to the genealogy was his attempt to make anti-humanism more concrete, more critical, more "political," as, for example, in his analysis of the extremely humble and concrete demands in prison revolts.

Central to Foucault's turn to genealogy was thus his attempt to analyze the connections between bodies of knowledge and techniques of domination, and to develop a new conception of critique in terms of revolt or resistance in such "knowledge-power." In his book on prisons, the problem of the historical constitution of the subject becomes a problem not simply about knowledge but about power, and not simply about discourse but about practice. When the problem of the subject is analyzed in terms of practice and power, then the issue of what to do about it also becomes a practical and political one. The result is to make anthropologism seem much more intractible than the forecast of its imminent demise could allow, but much less historically imposing in that as a practical issue, there is something we can do about it.

During the period in which he takes on Nietzche's genealogy, Foucault thus rethinks assumptions involving a confused notion of "politics" epitomized in what he comes to call the "negative" model of power. In rejecting uncritical reliance on the concept of power as exclusion or interdiction, he moves toward a concept of domination as a body of practical techniques to which knowledge is linked, and a concept of freedom not as that which domination excludes but as the possibility of practical revolt within it. Accordingly, he revises or rethinks the "politics" of his critique of psychiatry and his focus on discourse:

Many had found in his early work a kind of romanticism about madness, as though madness were a good-in-itself which had been alienated or excluded by the psychiatric practice whose emergence and transformations he had attempted to analyze. To the degree that madness was conceived as an area of freedom outside of psychiatry, the critique of psychiatry assumed nostalgic or apocalyptic forms. In moving to the conception of freedom as revolt within a set of practices, Foucault thus disowned these kinds of critique.

There had been a kind of "idealism" in focusing on discourse as the framework for a historical analysis of knowledge. However, when Foucault begins to insist on the importance of practice, he correspondingly repudiates language either as a model or an object in that analysis. In particular, the stress on discourse had failed to appreciate obvious historical facts about the new "sciences of man" in our period—their relation with new kinds of "policy," new kinds of action, new ways of going about things. Indeed we find explicit philosophical notice of that change in Comte, Marx, and Dewey—philosophies in which knowledge is conceived not as an epistemic ordering of experience or discourse, but as something we do, a collective action, a "form of life." It is here that we find the philosophical attempts to replace "warranted assertability" for truth, and the research community for the Cartesian "spectator."

In turning to Nietzsche and genealogy, Foucault applies such a "practical" conception of knowledge to the question of the constitution of the subject. He comes to analyze the human sciences not simply as bodies of discourse but as great sprawling ways of doing things which define who we are in new ways, require new kinds of participation from us, and eventually change the nature of the state. The concept of practice thus introduces a new politics of knowledge which the discursive idealism of his earlier work had not allowed him to analyze.

Genealogy turns the problem of knowledge into a problem about power and freedom: truth becomes a "thing of this world . . . [that] induces regular effects of power." "The political question is not error, illusion, alienated consciousness or ideology; it is truth itself. Hence the importance of Nietzsche."[9]

Nietzsche's own *Genealogy* supplies a model for the "politics" of the true discourse in which we ourselves figure and participate. It introduces a nominalism: not to accept a particular moral psychology as given, but to analyze the practice through which people are brought to accept and apply it. Thus Foucault is engaged in "genealogy" when he analyzes the Christian concept of the flesh or the Cartesian concept of the *cogito* within the context of practices of confession and meditation, or when he analyzes the concept of the individual within the context of the individualizing practices of the disciplines.

Genealogy thus introduces the problem of how, by becoming constituted as subjects, we come to be subject*ed* within a configuration of practice. And, therefore, at the same time, it introduces the politics of the *freedom* we also have to criticize those very practices. "Gay science" is the critique that nominalizes and so frees us with respect to forms of experience presented as universal, natural or otherwise "grounded." Thus, when Foucault says "Nietzsche is the philosopher of power, a philosopher who managed to think of power without having to confine himself within a political theory to do so,"[10] he does not have in mind Nietzsche's actual political views or pronouncements. To conceive of power without a political theory is to introduce a new kind of political problem and a new kind of political role for philosophy:

1. Where classical political theory had asked how sovereignty is constituted *from* subjects, genealogy asks what the political consequences are of our being constituted *as* subjects. Nietzsche introduces a philosophy not of the state and its apparatuses but of the forms of our "self-government."

2. Where the aim of political theory has been to provide a philosophical foundation for the political order (actual or to be realized), Nietzsche introduces an analysis of those forms of self-government which have *no* foundation or are historically contingent.

3. Where political theory had given rise to a "scientific" analysis of political institutions, genealogy analyzes the politics of true discourse about those institutions. Thus, for example, Foucault looks for the sources of the science the nineteenth century called "political economy" in practices of administration and the control of poverty.

In short, the "politics" of genealogical philosophy is not the critique of the state and its institutions, but the critical opening of new ways of thinking about ourselves and our experience which no state can ignore.

This "politics of truth," this political anti-humanism, however, is not at all an anti-enlightenment nostalgia or an irrationalist rejection of modern democratic society, behind which lies the sort of Romanticism Nazi ideology exploited.

The kind of freedom to which it appeals is *incompatible* with the Romantic ideal of securing a fixed position within a seamless social totality.

Nietzsche was a fiercely unsystematic thinker and attracted a most varied sort of following. One use of his philosophy was to contribute to the development of a historical model that played a crucial role in German sociology from Tönnes to Weber—the model that links rationalization to modernization and contrasts them with holistic traditional societies. It was thus possible to reinterpret the philosophy of knowledge within a framework that pairs reason with modernity and unreason with tradition; Lukács, for example, discusses Nietzsche in such terms. In this framework Nietzsche's questioning of the will-to-knowledge appears as a rejection of modern enlightened society inducing a reactionary nostalgia for traditional ones. In fact, Foucault's own genealogy has been confused with such anti-modernism and irrationalism.

But in challenging the conception of reason as systematic ground, Foucault does not believe he is rejecting modern democratic or economic institutions. He does not interpret Nietzsche's analysis of the will-to-knowledge within the sociological framework of modern and traditional society. He does not (and thinks Nietzschean philosophy need not) take *sides* in the great German sociological debate about modernity and reason, but rather he questions the very *terms* in which the debate has been carried on.

To analyze the will-to-knowledge is not to oppose modern society as a whole. And yet one is entitled to ask about the historical role of a theory that understands modernization in terms of the progress of universal reason. As an actual historical hypothesis, modernization theory had had to cope with an increasing number of anomalies. But as a "philosophy" it has played a role in the imperial attempts to spread the development of Western Reason throughout the globe; it has contributed to the picture of Reason as a unified good it is the burden of white men or the duty of communists to implant everywhere. Foucault is claiming that we can give up *that* conception of Reason without losing all rational thought, destroying our democratic institutions, or ruining our economies.

Foucault reads Nietzsche's assaults on the "unconditionality" and "universality" of the will-to-knowledge not as a rejection of reason and modernity or a reduction of all knowledge to political manipulation, but as a use of history which does not credit philosophy with being its moral arbitrator or agent. There is no one unified universal form of reason, but what there *is* is a complex history of our participation in the practices that secure objectivity. Nietzsche's philosophy directs us to the political and philosophical importance of that history.

For Foucault, the "will" in the "will-to-knowledge" is therefore not constitutive agency. It is not the will of a people, a nation, or a race. It is many people acting and struggling with each other at once some dominating others, within a tacit system of action. There are many different such wills; to analyze the "will-to-knowledge" is to analyze how they emerge and are transformed. Freedom is thus not the agency of Reason in History; it is struggle within the "politics of truth" of the knowledge about us.

Nietzsche is the philosopher who separates the problem of freedom from the problem of acquiring the truth about ourselves, who would free us from the tyrannies of such truths through an analysis of their histories. He separates our freedom from the knowledge of our nature. Foucault's genealogy is a continuation of that philosophy.

The Question of Freedom

The question of freedom is one Foucault constantly, if tacitly, poses. It does not figure prominently either in his own presentations of his work or in the secondary literature about it. Yet I wish to argue that it is found in what he *does,* motivated by his search for a new role for philosophy in the "ethic of the intellectual." The question of freedom is found in his displacement of Kantian foundationalist questions toward a critical analysis of our objectification and subjectification. It is found in his "archaeologizing" of the problem of finitude. It is found in his "genealogical" definition of a politics of truth. His very use of history to problematize the subject raises a question about freedom.

Foucault invents a philosophy which would "free" our experience of ourselves or our subjectivity. He attempts to transform the interrelations, deeply rooted in our philosophical tradition, between conceptions of freedom and conceptions of truth, to provide an analysis for the problematization of subjectivity in modern experience.

In order to extract the central thesis of this new kind of philosophy, we must draw a distinction between real and nominal freedom. For every instituted conception of freedom we apply a nominalist reversal, and attempt to determine the larger practice within which it figures; that practice is then what involves our "real" freedom, something asocial which cannot be instituted or guaranteed. Thus our real freedom does not consist either in telling our true stories and finding our place within some tradition or ethical code, in completely determining our actions in accordance with universal principles, or in accepting our existential limitations in authentic self-relation. We are, on the contrary, "really" free because we can identify and change those procedures or forms through which our stories become true, because we can question and modify those systems which make (only) particular kinds of action possible, and because there is no "authentic" self-relation we must conform to.

Formally guaranteed freedoms always figure within some contingent historical practice; that practice is "political" in the sense that it imposes aims which we are really free to analyze, contest, and change. Formal freedoms are the nominal elements within a system of action our real freedom makes possible. If utopian thought has been the dream of a world in which our formal freedoms would become real, nominalist history contributes to our real freedom in exposing the nominal nature of our formal ones. Such history *is* therefore an active challenge to anthropologism. Anthropology entails that we are free because we have a nature that is real or one we must realize; nominalist history assumes that our "nature" in fact consists in just those features of ourselves by reference to which we are sorted into polities or groups. Our real freedom is found in dissolving or changing the polities that embody our nature, and as such it is asocial or anarchical. No society or polity *could* be based on it, since it lies precisely in the possibility of constant change. Our real freedom is thus political, though it is never finalizable, legislatable, or rooted in our nature.

Foucault's philosophy is the critical appeal to this real freedom. Its "truth" is therefore different in kind from the truths of science. Research in philosophy becomes more than a systematic collection of knowledge. It is a *critique* which does not attempt to fix the foundations for knowledge, to provide theory with a justification, or to defend Reason, but to occasion new ways of thinking. It analyzes how knowledge about ourselves is tied up in complex ways with techniques of domination, and sees freedom not as the end of domination or as our removal from history, but rather as the revolt through which history may constantly be changed. Foucault's philosophy is thus neither prescriptive nor merely descriptive. It is occasion, spark, challenge. It is risk; it is not guaranteed, backed-up, or assured: it always remains without an end.

Because it cannot be guaranteed or established, such philosophy has a singular political and intellectual role. Its freedom requires a more complex politics than, for example, the guarantee of the "freedom of speech" in democratic societies. Its truth is more than obedience to rational standards; it does not consist in articulating the voice of a people or in providing for the administration of their happiness or welfare. Philosophy is that "free thought" which government cannot prescribe and whose truth it cannot turn into law.

Intellectually and politically it is oriented toward the existence of concrete controversy, conflict, debate, paradox surrounding subjectivity: in the demands of prison revolts, the objections to psychiatric institutions, the claims of sexual "deviants," and in the politics of modernist and post-modernist cultural forms.

"Humanist" philosophies have attempted to understand the problem of subjectivity in a foundational mode that introduces models of the alienation or repression of an authentic philosophically guaranteed subjectivity. Foucault's "anti-humanist" philosophy rather understands the problematization of subjectivity in historical terms as an issue about our real and not our foundational freedom. It attempts to replace the model of the unrepressed Freudian subject and the unalienated Marxist subject with a "Nietzschean" model of the nonfinalized problematization of the forms through which the experience of the subject is constituted.

Foucault thus proposes a new function and ethic for the intellectual. It is not the attempt to find an authenticity of self-experience in which to anchor one's choices, projects, or artistic work, but the attempt to constantly question the "truth" of one's thought and oneself. It requires the invention of new modes of thought and of action. It is the ethic of what Foucault calls *se déprendre de soi-même:*[11] the constant questioning and transforming of the role of one's "self" in one's thought.

Foucault invents a philosophy not of foundation but of risk; a philosophy that is the endless question of freedom.

Notes

1. See Foucault, *L'Usage des plaisirs,* p. 15: "Il y a toujours quelque chose de dérisoire dans le discours philosophique lorsqu'il veut, de 'l'extérieur, faire la loi aux autres, leur dire où est leur vérité, et comment la trouver, ou lorsqu'il se fait fort d'instruire leur proces en postivité naive; mais, c'est son droit d'explorer ce qui, dans sa propre pensée, peut etre changé par l'excercise qu'il fait d'un savoir qui lui est étranger." ("There is always something foolish about philosophical discourse when it wants to impose the law on others from the outside, tell them where their truth lies, and how to find it, or when it strengthens itself by teaching them about the naive positivity of their processes; but it is its right to examine what in its own thought can be changed through the exercise it makes of a knowledge foreign to it.")
2. Foucault, "Georges Canguilhem: Philosopher of Error."
3. *Ibid.*
4. Foucault, *The Order of Things,* p. 342.
5. Ian Hacking, "Foucault's Immature Science," *Nous* (1979), no. 13.
6. Foucault, "Georges Canguilhem: Philosopher of Error."
1. See Foucault, *L'Usage des plaisirs,* p. 15: "Il y a toujours quelque chose de dérisoire dans le discours philosophique lorsqu'il veut, de 'l'extérieur, faire la loi aux autres, leur dire où est leur vérité, et comment la trouver, ou lorsqu'il se fait fort d'instruire leur proces en postivité naive; mais, c'est son droit d'explorer ce qui, dans sa propre pensée, peut etre changé par l'excercise qu'il fait d'un savoir qui lui est étranger." ("There is always something foolish about philosophical discourse when it wants to impose the law on others from the outside, tell them where their truth lies, and how to find it, or when it strengthens itself by teaching them about the naive positivity of their processes; but it is its right to examine what in its own thought can be changed through the exercise it makes of a knowledge foreign to it.")
2. Foucault, "Georges Canguilhem: Philosopher of Error."
3. *Ibid.*
4. Foucault, *The Order of Things,* p. 342.
5. Ian Hacking, "Foucault's Immature Science," *Nous* (1979), no. 13.
6. Foucault, "Georges Canguilhem: Philosopher of Error."

7. Foucault, *The Order of Things,* p. 341. Hereafter page numbers given parenthetically in the text.

8. Henri Birault, *Heidegger et l'expérience de la pensée* (Paris: Gallimard, 1978), pp. 445ff.

9. Foucault, *Power/Knowledge,* p. 133.

10. *Ibid.,* p. 53.

11. See Foucault, *L'Usage des plaisirs,* p. 15.

Foucault's Writings
Referred to in the Text

1962 "Introduction." Jean-Jacques Rousseau, *Dialogues*. Paris: A. Colin.

1963 *Raymond Roussel*. Paris: Gallimard.

1964 "La Folie, l'absence d'oeuvre." *La Table Ronde*, no. 196.

1966 *Les Mots et les choses*. Paris: Gallimard.

1969 *L'Archéologie du savoir*. Paris: Gallimard.

1970 *The Order of Things*. New York: Random House.

1972 *The Archaeology of Knowledge*. New York: Harper.

1975 *I, Pierre Rivière*. Frank Jellinek, tr. New York: Pantheon.

——— *Surveiller et punir*. Paris: Gallimard.

1977 *Discipline and Punish*. Alan Sheridan, tr. New York: Pantheon.

——— *Language, Counter-Memory, Practice*. Donald F. Bouchard, tr. Ithaca, N.Y.: Cornell University Press.

1978 *The History of Sexuality*. New York: Pantheon.

1979 "On Governmentality." *I & C*, no. 6, p. 22.

1980 *L'Impossible Prison*. Paris: Editions du Seuil.

——— *Power/Knowledge*. Colin Gordon, tr. New York: Pantheon.

1981 "Est-il donc important de penser?" *Libération* (Paris).

1980 "Georges Canguilhem: Philosopher of Error." *I & C*, no. 7, pp. 52–59.

1984 *L'Usage des plaisirs*. Paris: Gallimard.

Index